The TRAINING *SPIRAL*

The TRAINING SPIRAL

Traditional Methods Reimagined
for the 21st-Century Horse and Rider

TRAFALGAR SQUARE
North Pomfret, Vermont

Sue Grice

First published in 2023 by

Trafalgar Square Books
North Pomfret, Vermont 05053

Library of Congress Cataloging-in-Publication Data
Names: Grice, Sue, author.
Title: The training spiral : traditional methods reimagined for the
  21st-century horse and rider / Sue Grice.
Description: North Pomfret, Vermont : Trafalgar Square Books, 2022. |
  Includes index. | Summary: "Dressage rider and trainer Sue Grice grew up
  on the traditional "scales of training" or "training pyramid," used the
  world over to provide a standard system of progression for developing
  the equine athlete, and in particular dressage and event horses that are
  working toward a superior ability to "collect." The scales and pyramid
  are not only boring to many riders, they can be confusing when it comes
  to actually implementing them as guideposts, so Grice has conceived a
  system based on the standard but with a focus on a better rate of
  success. This success is achieved when the rider is engaged with the
  system and understands how to continually adhere to it, even as advances
  (or falters) occur"-- Provided by publisher.
Identifiers: LCCN 2022011143 (print) | LCCN 2022011144 (ebook) | ISBN
  9781646011278 (paperback) | ISBN 9781646011285 (epub)
Subjects: LCSH: Horses--Training.
Classification: LCC SF287 .G78 2022 (print) | LCC SF287 (ebook) | DDC
  636.1/0835--dc23/eng/20220713
LC record available at https://lccn.loc.gov/2022011143
LC ebook record available at https://lccn.loc.gov/2022011144

All photos by *Sue Grice* except: 6.7, 6.8, 6.14 *(Juma Photography)*;
6.12, 6.15, 7.25 C *(Stephen Hammond)*; 7.19 C, 7.24 B *(Dave Cameron)*; and 2.5 A–D, 6.2, 6.10
B, 6.13, 6.16 C, 6.17 B, 6.18, 7.21 B, 7.23 B, 7.25 B *(Linda Collis)*.
All illustrations by *Sue Grice*
Book design by *Katarzyna Misiukanis–Celińska (https://misiukanis-artstudio.com)*
Cover design by *RM Didier*
Typefaces: *PT Serif, Roboto* and *Courgette*
Index by *Andrea Jones (JonesLiteraryServices.com)*

Printed in China
10 9 8 7 6 5 4 3 2 1

MAY 2023

*I would like to dedicate this book
to all the wonderful horses
I have had the pleasure of working
with over the years, in particular
Sandy, Pingy, and Frodo
who have taught me so much
and given me so many opportunities.*

CONTENTS

THE TRAINING SPIRAL

INTROD

The clarity of my approach will also help your horse to understand what is being asked of him, leading ultimately to a happier relationship between horse and rider

"

UCTION

The so-called "Scales of Training" (Training Pyramid) are very well known in the equestrian world and feature in many books and manuals. However, if my 30-plus years' experience as an equestrian coach has taught me one thing, it is how much confusion surrounds this very familiar concept, among both riders and coaches. Most of this confusion is not about the Scales of Training per se, but about how they should be applied in practice—and particularly when each of the six elements of the Scales should be used. I have often been witness to the debates among coaches about, for example, whether the element of Straightness should come before Impulsion, or vice versa.

Over the course of a long career, I have developed my own framework for implementing the Scales of Training, and I believe it is one that avoids nearly all these problems. Describing and explaining this framework is the purpose of

THE TRAINING SPIRAL

INTROD

> *With a happier horse, a happier rider, and clarity of communication all around, training should progress more quickly and easily*

UCTION

this book. Although my approach is in some ways unique, the traditional concept of the Scales is not in any way being challenged. Rather, what I am proposing is a new way of visualizing and, thus, applying the Scales of Training: instead of the "pyramid" structure that is usually presented, I am suggesting that the Scales should be conceptualized as a *spiral*.

As I hope to show, the spiral structure provides a means of applying the Scales in practice that is not just logical and progressive but extremely easy to follow. This clear training structure will be of benefit to riders and coaches at all levels, from absolute novices up to the most experienced. The clarity of my approach will also help your horse to understand what is being asked of him, leading ultimately to a happier relationship between horse and rider. With a happier horse, a happier rider, and clarity of communication all around, training should progress more quickly and easily.

The Scales describe how a horse's training
should be developed over
a period of time-often a lengthy one.

chapter

1

What Are the Scales of Training?

1 ――――――――

The roots of the Scales of Training are thought to date back to the early twentieth century when German coaches devised a structure for the training of military horses. By the 1950s, a more detailed plan had been developed. This later scheme is the foundation of the Scales of Training that we are familiar with today.

Essentially, the Scales offer a progressive training guide. This is usually seen as having six elements: *Rhythm, Suppleness, Contact, Impulsion, Straightness,* and *Collection*. The individual elements will be explained in more detail in the pages that follow. The Scales are often represented as a pyramid structure (fig.1.1), with Rhythm as the foundation or starting point; Suppleness, Straightness, and so on as the intermediate ascending stages; and Collection as the peak, or final element of the Scales.

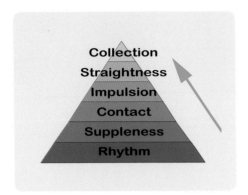

1.1

A traditional model of the Scales of Training, starting with Rhythm and finishing with Collection at the top level shown in a pyramid structure. ▲

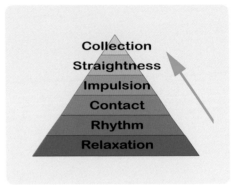

1.2

A variation of the Scales of Training, starting with Relaxation instead of Rhythm at the lower level of the pyramid. ▲

Over the years, there have been a number of variations on this basic model, with some trainers putting Straightness below (or before) Impulsion, on the grounds that the horse cannot produce Impulsion unless he is straight. Another common variant has Relaxation as the starting point and makes no mention of Suppleness (fig. 1.2).

Many trainers divide the six elements into three main phases. In this concept, the first two levels of the pyramid (which, in the form I will be using, are Rhythm and Suppleness) make up the *familiarization* phase—that is, the stage at which the horse is *building his confidence and understanding.* Then come the middle two stages, Contact and Impulsion, when the horse acquires his *pushing power.*

Finally, the top two levels of the pyramid, Straightness and Collection, see the horse develop *carrying power.* So now we have a conceptual model that looks like the one in Figure 1.3.

Other variations that have been developed often aim to show the links or points of connection between the elements.

For all these variants, the general understanding of the Scales remains fairly constant. The training of a young or inexperienced horse begins with the establishment of Rhythm and Suppleness (or Relaxation); then, as training progresses, we move on to develop the quality of his acceptance of the aids (Contact), and then add exercises to build up strength and energy (Impulsion). Finally, in the last stages of training, the horse will develop Straightness and be able to work in Collection.

In other words, the Scales describe how a horse's training should be developed over a period of time—often

6 ___

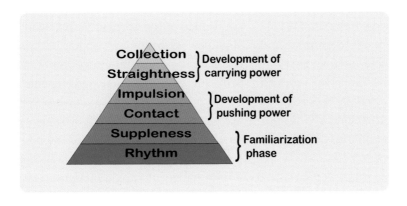

1.3

Traditional Scales of Training model showing the three major phases of training. ▲

a lengthy one. The pyramid concept is linear in structure and implies quite strongly that you should only move up a level once the lower level has been mastered; for example, you should not focus on Contact until Suppleness has been achieved, and Rhythm should be mastered before moving on to Suppleness.

There is nothing wrong with this development path and I have no wish to quarrel with it. In practice, however, things are not often so simple. One element of the Scales can have a strong influence upon another, so that the training of a horse is not achieved in the straightforward linear fashion that the model seems to imply. Indeed, I will go further and suggest that the Scales, with all their elements, can be used systematically during an individual training session, at any level.

The model put forward in this book—the *Training Spiral* approach—is suitable for horses at the very beginning of their career, as well as those at advanced levels of training. It is, likewise, appropriate for all standards of rider, from novices to the most experienced.

★ The Individual Elements

As previously noted, there are differing opinions as to which elements should be included in the Scales of Training. A good argument can be made for each version. However, the purpose of this book is not to examine and choose between these variants, but rather to describe a new framework in which any of them can potentially be placed. For present purposes, therefore, we will stick to the most commonly used elements:

- Rhythm
- Suppleness
- Contact
- Impulsion
- Straightness
- Collection

Although Relaxation is not included in the scheme, it is a very important part of a horse's training and will not be overlooked.

As a further caveat, it should be noted that the individual elements are often interpreted in slightly different ways. To some extent, this is because the English names for the elements were all originally translated from German, and certain nuances of meaning have been lost in the process. For example, the German name for the element that we call Contact is *Anlehnung*, which literally translates as "following." Similarly, the German word *Geraderichten* translates to "straightening," rather than "straightness," and one could argue that there is a significant difference between the two. In the case of the final element, Collection, a better

translation of the German *Versammlung* would be "assembly," which has a sense of "bringing everything together" that is missing from the usual English name.

In the notes that follow, I give a brief account of each of the standard elements as I have interpreted them for the purposes of this book. That is not to say that an alternative interpretation is incorrect; simply that this is the meaning I have chosen to use here. One could easily write a book on each of the six elements. However, my aim is not to make the reader an expert on the elements of training, but rather to provide enough information about each to facilitate the understanding of the Training Spiral concept.

Rhythm

Rhythm refers to the regular beat of the horse's footfalls.

In *walk,* the rhythm should be a clear four beats (1, 2, 3, 4) with each beat equally spaced as in a marching rhythm.

In *trot,* the rhythm should be a clear two beats, and in *canter,* it should be three beats with a short pause when the horse is in mid-air on completion of the stride (the "moment of suspension").

I will not go into great detail here about the footfalls in each gait, as it is enough to understand that the beat in every case should be regular, as should the tempo (speed of the beat). In other words, there should be no speeding up or slowing down, and the horse should not lose the regularity of the beat as he works.

There are times when a horse can lose this regularity—for example, when he goes into what is known as a "lateral walk." In this case, the beat becomes 1, 2...3, 4 instead of the regular 1, 2, 3, 4. While there can be many causes for such loss of rhythm, a key factor to consider at this stage is lack of Relaxation. If a horse is not feeling relaxed, then the quality of his rhythm will often suffer as a result.

This is one reason why the Scales of Training are often given with Relaxation as the foundation element. However, in this book I am going to consider Relaxation alongside Rhythm.

Suppleness

Suppleness refers to the state of the horse's muscles and the capacity to stretch and contract them. Often people confuse Suppleness with the horse's ability to bend around a corner. Of course, the horse does need a degree of suppleness in his body to be able to do this; yet the quality of bend is a different issue, and one that can be covered more appropriately when we get to the element of Straightness (see p. 11).

A tense horse will have tight muscles and this limits his ability to perform the movements asked of him. A supple horse is one that can easily stretch and contract his muscles so that his body can assume the different positions with ease. For example, the horse should find it easy to lift his back and raise and arch his neck into a "working outline"—and equally easy to stretch his neck long and low and to stretch out over his back.

For a horse to be supple he must be relaxed, as any tension he has will impact his Suppleness. Hence Relaxation and a good Rhythm should be achieved prior to working on Suppleness.

Contact

Contact is often referred to more explicitly as "acceptance of the Contact." For most trainers, this means primarily the contact between

the rider's hands and the horse's mouth, via the bit and reins. The aim is that the horse should be soft, accepting of this contact and, importantly, also going forward toward the bit as though he is actively seeking it. If this is what we want from the horse with regards to the rein contact, the same applies to the contact of the rider's legs and seat to the horse's back and sides.

Does the horse accept the rider's leg? Some horses have a tendency to block against the rider's leg when a leg aid is applied, and some will run away from the rider's leg aids. Ideally, you would like the horse to be soft, accepting, and reactive to the rider's leg and seat aids in just the same way that we would like him to be soft, accepting, and reactive in the rein contact.

Impulsion

Impulsion can be thought of as an addition of energy to the way in which the horse is working. This extra energy should come from the horse's hindquarters as he starts to push himself up off the ground and forward with increased power. The additional power should travel through the horse's body from the hind legs and forward to the nose without tension or resistance.

It is worth noting that Impulsion is not directly connected to speed. It is often thought that the faster a horse is traveling, the more Impulsion he must have.

1.4

This horse is clearly working on two tracks with the hind legs following in the same tracks as the front legs. ▲

1.5

Looking at this horse from above, you can see how the blue line shows the alignment of the spine from his ears to his tail is an equal curve all the way along. He is well aligned or "straight." ▲

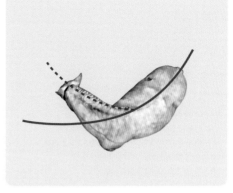

1.6

In this picture, you can see how the horse's neck is bending much more than the rest of his body, and, as such, he is not equally aligned through his whole spine so he is not "straight." ▲

This is not necessarily so: a horse that is trotting fast from one end of the arena to the other may simply be pulling himself along with his front legs or pushing himself out of balance and falling forward. Conversely, a horse in a very collected trot may take twice as long to get from one end of the arena to the other but have much higher levels of Impulsion as he is using a lot of power to carry his body and has much contained energy within it.

Straightness

Straightness refers to how the horse's body is aligned from front to back.

When traveling in a straight line, a "straight" horse will appear to be moving on two distinct tracks, with the left hind leg following the same line as the left front leg, and the right hind leg following the same line as the right front leg (fig. 1.4).

When the horse is moving on a curved line, the curvature of his spine should be equal from nose to tail, as shown in Figure 1.5. By contrast in Figure 1.6, you see more neck bend than body bend and this horse is not "straight."

Understandably, people often get confused by the idea of Straightness when it is applied to a horse moving on a circle. A much better word to describe straightness on a circle is "alignment."

When a horse is traveling on a circle, you want his body to be aligned along the curve of the circle so that the left hind leg follows the same curved line as the left front leg, and the right hind leg follows the same curved line as the right front leg (fig. 1.7). To achieve this, the horse's spine should follow the curvature of the circle.

Collection

At its simplest, Collection is the horse's ability to take more of his body's weight onto his hindquarters. A horse at the

1.7

This horse is bending on a curved line and his left hind leg is following in the same line (pink) as his left front leg and his right hind leg is following in the same line (yellow) as his right front leg. ▼

beginning of his training will often be "on the forehand"—that is, he carries too much of his weight on his front legs. As his training progresses, he will develop more ability to lighten the forehand and lower and engage his hindquarters, thus creating a more uphill effect (fig. 1.8). Of course, it should be noted that some horses are naturally more uphill in their way of working than others due to their conformation.

Collection is often seen less as an exercise in its own right and more as a product of all the previous elements working together. As I have noted, this idea is reflected in the original German term *Versammlung*, which translates to "assembly." Assembling all the previous five elements creates Collection.

A Note on Balance

Balance is not recognized as a specific element in the Scales of Training, yet it is

1.8

On the left, you see a novice horse whose frame is in a downhill direction because he is carrying his weight with his front legs. On the right, you see an advanced horse that is now able to carry his weight much more with his hind legs, and the result is he carries himself in a more uphill frame. ▲

TERMS AND LEVELS

The terms used across countries for the different stages a horse may be training or competing at vary, so below I have included a chart that outlines these terms, along with an example of the type of movements expected at each stage, for the United States, United Kingdom, and Germany.

In this book I use the official levels of the United States Dressage Federation (USDF). Note that throughout the book I do often make reference to "novice" and "advanced" horses, but I am using these as generic terms: I consider a "novice horse" one who can perform movements such as the walk, trot, and canter, 15- and 20-meter circles, and three-looped serpentines. An "advanced horse" in this book can perform more complex movements such as flying changes and canter pirouettes.

The United States	The United Kingdom	Germany	Examples of movements expected
Introductory Level	Introductory		Walk, trot, 20-meter circles
Training Level	Preliminary	E	Walk, trot, canter, 20-meter circles
First Level	Novice	A*, A**	Medium trot and canter, 15-meter circles
Second Level	Elementary	L*, LL*	Leg-yield, shoulder-in, 10-meter circles
Third Level	Medium and Advanced Medium	M*, M^^	Half-pass, single flying change
Fourth Level	Advanced	S*	Tempi changes
Prix St. Georges	Prix St. Georges	S**	Half-canter pirouette, canter single zigzag
Intermediate I & II	Intermediate I & II	S***	Two-time flying changes, full canter pirouettes
Grand Prix	Grand Prix	Grand Prix	Piaffe, passage, one-time changes, canter zigzags

something that riders and trainers refer to all the time. For example, a trainer may well ask a rider to "rebalance" the horse when they are going around a corner. A horse can show good or poor balance within any and all movements, for example, while executing a collected canter, an extended trot, a halt on the centerline, or while trotting a 20-meter circle. So, it is worth taking a moment to consider balance. *Are balance and Collection the same thing*? Well, no, not quite—although, like Collection, balance is less a quality in its own right and more a product of various other elements all being in place.

A horse can lose his balance for many reasons. For example, he could lose his Suppleness, which causes him to brace one side of his body, which in turn causes him to fall in and thus lose balance. Or, perhaps, he loses the softness of his forward acceptance of the rein Contact and begins to lean on the rein, which causes him to fall forward and run onto his forehand, again losing balance.

More often than not, if you take a moment to consider the cause of the loss of balance, you will find that it relates to the loss of one of the elements of the Scales of Training. Hence, when a rider successfully "rebalances" her horse, this is usually done by "fixing" the element in question. For example, if the horse loses his Suppleness to the inside and he becomes braced in his body, the rider can nudge the horse "off" or around her inside leg in order to regain the suppleness in the horse's body, thus allowing the horse to recover his balance.

end of chapter 1

What Are the Scales of Training?

> *The Scales used in training*
> *a horse should be more like the gentle gradations*
> *or tiers of a spiral.*

chapter

2

The Training Spiral: The Scales of Training Remodeled

2 ——————————

Although the traditional pyramid concept of the Scales of Training clearly has a place within equestrianism, it is my contention that it does not provide the most helpful framework for applying the elements of the Scales. In the following pages I would like to propose a different model—a *Training Spiral.*

Before going any further, consider for a moment what the word "scale" actually means. It has various meanings in the English language, including:

- A set of marks or numbers used to measure the size or level of something.

- The relation between the real size of something and its size on a map or model.

- The relative level or extent of something.

- A machine or device for weighing people or things.

- A set of musical notes played in ascending or descending order.

- To climb something steep, such as a mountain or ladder.

2.1

The conceptual model of the Training Spiral. Each of the different colors represents a different element of the six Scales of Training. At the bottom, you can see a horse just starting his training and at the top, a horse who has had much training. ▲

While some of these meanings may appear irrelevant to training horses, all are worth a little thought. Most obviously, the idea of "scaling" something steep via a series of steps fits well with the pyramid structure set out in the last chapter. The notion of a scale as a means of measuring something, such as progress or attainment, also seems appropriate. If you open a thesaurus and look up synonyms for the word "scales," you will find some more interesting terms: *balances, gauges, measures, gradations, hierarchies, tiers.*

In my view, the scales used in training a horse should be more like the gentle gradations or tiers of a spiral than a series of steps leading straight up from the base to the peak of a pyramid. The idea of "scales" of music—often undertaken as a practice exercise—is also very suggestive. The spiral model that I propose is based upon the traditional Scales of Training but enables a more gradual progression from one tier to the next, as the horse's training proceeds.

The basic idea of the Training Spiral is that you can progress through all the elements of the Scales in order (Rhythm, Suppleness, Contact, Impulsion, Straightness, Collection), without having to *perfect* each one before attempting the next. Instead, each element is completed to the degree that the horse can manage at his given level of training. As soon as one *cycle* of this training—one tier of the spiral—is completed, the next can begin—only in this new cycle (Tier 2), the degree of difficulty or quality expected is increased. This process will be explained in more detail, beginning on p. 33, but the basic concept of the spiral shape is shown in Figure 2.2.

Riders of all levels and with different aims and ambitions can utilize the Training Spiral as it is applicable to anyone seeking to improve their horse's way of going, even if they are not aiming as high as Grand Prix and even if they focus on a horse sport other than dressage. The Training Spiral can be applied over many different time frames—for example, over a five-minute section of a single training session, or over the period of a week's

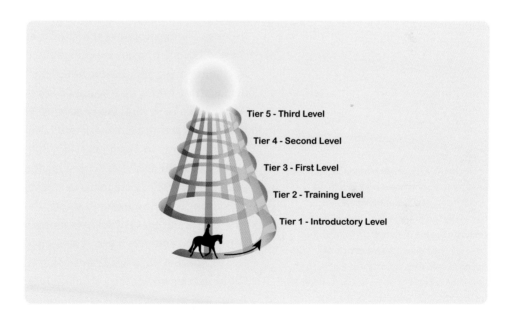

Tier 5 - Third Level

Tier 4 - Second Level

Tier 3 - First Level

Tier 2 - Training Level

Tier 1 - Introductory Level

2.2

A Training Spiral showing how a horse at Introductory Level may start at Tier 1, working on Rhythm (indicated as the red band), and progress up the tiers of the Spiral as he works toward Third Level. At Third Level, he may have completed five tiers on this Spiral, which would have likely taken him several years to complete. ▲

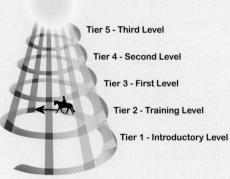

Tier 5 - Third Level

Tier 4 - Second Level

Tier 3 - First Level

Tier 2 - Training Level

Tier 1 - Introductory Level

2.3 A–C

In Figure (A) you can see how our Introductory Level horse from Figure 2.2 is still on the first tier of the Spiral but has moved on to working on Impulsion (indicated as the green band). Even further on in his education (B), the horse is at Second Level in his training and the fourth tier of the spiral. The horse is now working on Rhythm again (indicated by the red band), but at a much higher level than when on previous tiers. At this level it is expected that the Rhythm is maintained while performing more challenging exercises. Finally, the horse reaches Tier 5 of the Spiral, and Third Level (C)! ▲

training, or over the course of months of training. The application of the Spiral over these different time scales is explained in chapter 3 (p. 34), but for now, I will demonstrate how it may be applied over a time scale of several years, assuming a horse is starting at Introductory Level and progressing to Third Level (fig. 2.2).

In the Spiral, each tier represents the progression of the horse to his next level of training. In our current example, the first tier represents the horse's journey through Introductory Level, the second tier his journey through Training Level, the third tier his journey through First Level, and so on until he is at the "top" of the Spiral, which in this case is Third Level.

Here we can see how the horse begins at the bottom of the Spiral at Introductory Level (see fig. 2.2) and, as his training progresses, he moves up the tiers of the

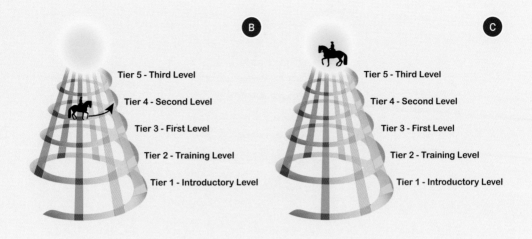

spiral (figs. 2.3 A–C), improving each of the six elements of the scales of training in the following order (Rhythm, Suppleness, Contact, Impulsion, Straightness, Collection) to an *acceptable degree for the stage the horse is training at*, before progressing to the next tier. There he will *again* work to improve each of the six elements (in order), but this time to a higher degree of quality than he did in the previous tier. This process is repeated again and again as the horse gradually improves and progresses by focusing on each of the elements of the Scales of Training, one at a time, and at an appropriate degree of difficulty for his level. In the case of the Introductory Level horse, each tier might take perhaps a year or so to establish to a satisfactory standard before progressing on to the next tier as horse and rider progress to Third Level.

To repeat, at each level of the Spiral, the horse should be able to achieve a degree of Rhythm, Suppleness, Contact, Impulsion, Straightness, and Collection *appropriate for the horse's stage of training*. Obviously, the degree of difficulty or quality expected is different at each level. For example, the degree of Collection shown by a horse at the Introductory Level may simply be that he is no longer "diving" onto his forehand, whereas when a horse is trained to a more advanced level, such as Grand Prix, you expect to see a much higher degree of Collection—for example, the ability to perform passage and piaffe (fig. 2.4). The sequences of photographs on these pages demonstrate how this process of becoming more collected is an incremental development *throughout* the horse's training and not just something that is only relevant to horses at an advanced stage of

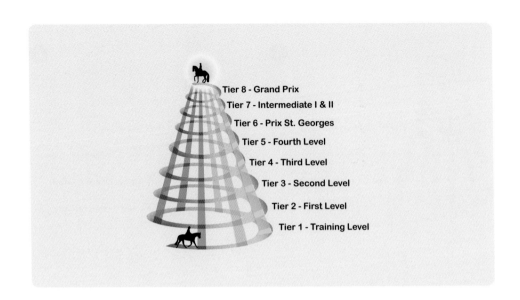

Tier 8 - Grand Prix

Tier 7 - Intermediate I & II

Tier 6 - Prix St. Georges

Tier 5 - Fourth Level

Tier 4 - Third Level

Tier 3 - Second Level

Tier 2 - First Level

Tier 1 - Training Level

2.4

A Training Spiral showing eight tiers, starting at Training Level and progressing up to Grand Prix Level. ▲

training (figs. 2.5 A–D). As you look at the photographs, visualize a Spiral that spans many years and shows the horse's progress from Training Level up to Grand Prix Level (see fig. 2.4 for an example), and consider where each horse would be on it.

The sequence of images not only shows the incremental progression of collection but also demonstrates how even horses that have not been bred for high performance (in this case, three pony breeds!) can, with correct training, achieve higher-level dressage movements, such as piaffe, where a high degree of collection is required. Of course, Warmbloods that have been specifically bred for movement and athleticism can often perform the higher-level movements with more ease and expression. However, we should never allow any prejudices against the

2.5 A–D

In (A), you see a Highland Pony working at Training Level (Tier 1 on the Spiral shown in fig. 2.4).
He is at the early stages of his training, and you can see how he is still inclined to work in a downhill
frame. In (B), we see the same Highland Pony several years later, now training at Second Level
(Tier 3 on the Spiral shown in fig. 2.4). He is carrying more weight with his hind legs, thus producing
a more uphill frame. In (C) is another British native pony who has progressed in his training to Third
Level (Tier 4 on the Spiral shown in fig. 2.4) and is able to engage his hindquarters to take more of his
weight behind. Photo (D) is a Connemara pony who is just progressing to the highest levels
of training and starting to piaffe (Tier 7 on the Spiral shown in fig. 2.4). The additional engagement
of the hindquarters is clear to see. ▲

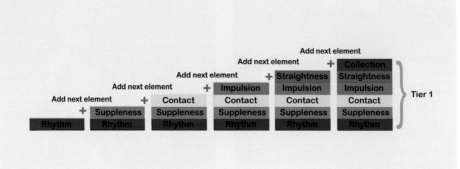

Add next element

Add next element

Add next element

Add next element

Add next element

					Collection
				Straightness	Straightness
			Impulsion	Impulsion	Impulsion
		Contact	Contact	Contact	Contact
	Suppleness	Suppleness	Suppleness	Suppleness	Suppleness
Rhythm	Rhythm	Rhythm	Rhythm	Rhythm	Rhythm

Tier 1

non-typical dressage horse (or pony) to cause us to predetermine the level to which they may progress.

Whatever your horse's breed and whatever your discipline, the aim should be that at each tier of the Training Spiral the six elements of the Scales become increasingly accomplished, and the horse able to perform more difficult movements and exercises while still maintaining the quality in each of the elements. Consider again the horse training over a period of years (see fig. 2.2, p. 19). Perhaps on the first tier the horse is at Training Level—his degree of Impulsion should be enough for him to perform a forward and fluid working trot to working canter transition, and he should be able to maintain a working canter. However, the degree of Impulsion required when he is on Tier 4 of the Spiral (in our example on p. 22, now training at Third Level) we would expect *more* Impulsion (when compared to the degree of Impulsion he had in Tier 1) so he can perform more challenging movements, such as transitions from walk to canter and working canter to medium canter. The same is true for each other element, at each tier of the Spiral. As the horse progresses up the Spiral an improvement in each element should be observed. This may be in terms of the horse being able to maintain a Rhythm

2.6

The Training Tower being built with one element ("brick") added at a time to form Tier 1. The single tier of the Tower is equivalent to one tier of the Training Spiral. ▲

or quality of Contact, or it could be that the horse becomes more athletic (for example in his Suppleness and Impulsion).

★ *An Alternative Visualization*

An alternative way of visualizing this training system is to think of a *Tower* structure (fig. 2.6). The basic principle of the Tower is the same as the Spiral in that a sufficient degree of accomplishment should be shown in each element before moving on and adding the next element, which I picture as "adding bricks" to make a taller tower (fig. 2.7).

If we compare the Tower concept to the Spiral shown in Figure 2.4 (p. 22) where the first tier represented the horse at Training Level, then Tier 1 of the Tower would also represent the horse's development through Training Level where he should develop a sufficient degree of the six "bricks" (Rhythm, Suppleness, Contact, Impulsion, Straightness, and Collection) to perform all the movements required at that level. I find the two visualizations— both the Spiral and the Tower—equally useful in describing the training process (as you will see later on—see p. 25).

At first glance the Tower concept may seem very similar to the traditional pyramid structure with each element "built upon" the previous elements; however, in the pyramid structure, it is generally thought that once you reach Collection,

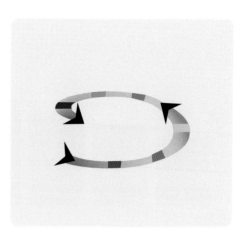

2.7

Here you see one tier of the Training Spiral, with each color marked on to represent one element of the Scales of Training, and each color equivalent to one "brick" in the Tower. ▲

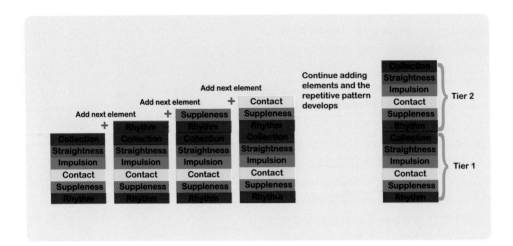

Add next element $+$

Add next element $+$

Add next element $+$

| Collection |
| Straightness |
| Impulsion |
| Contact |
| Suppleness |
| Rhythm |

Continue adding elements and the repetitive pattern develops

| Collection |
| Straightness |
| Impulsion |
| Contact |
| Suppleness |
| Rhythm |
Tier 2

| Collection |
| Straightness |
| Impulsion |
| Contact |
| Suppleness |
| Rhythm |
Tier 1

2.8

As with the Spiral, each element is added one at a time, and a new tier builds on top of the one that was previously completed. ▲

that is the end—you are at the top of the pyramid. In both the Spiral and the Tower structures, there are an *infinite* number of tiers. You may never reach a "top" where your horse stops confirming and improving the elements. You can always go on to spiral higher or build the Tower higher, layering on top of what you have already done. Tier 2 of the Tower is the equivalent to Tier 2 of the Spiral, but it is two tiers high and contains a total of 12 "bricks" (figs. 2.8 and 2.9).

When you look at the degree of quality in each element in the first tier in comparison to the degree of quality in the second tier, there should be an improvement. In the first tier, the horse may be able to maintain a good Rhythm through a three-loop serpentine but loses his Rhythm when attempting a four-loop serpentine. By the second tier, he is able to maintain a good Rhythm in a four-loop serpentine. Why? Because his Suppleness, Contact, Impulsion, Straightness, and Collection all improved during the journey through the first tier!

I think, partly because of the traditional pyramid structure most of us are so familiar with, people often think of Collection as something that only happens in horses that are at a very advanced stage of training. However, as I've already illustrated on page 21, degrees of Collection are evident at *all* stages of a horse's training. While he may not be able to perform an advanced movement, when we watch him working, we would still see a small shift in balance so he is carrying slightly more weight behind (in other words, an increased degree of Collection).

The principle of the tiers is simple and rather like playing musical scales on a piano—the pianist plays one set of notes (for example, C to B) before repeating the same sequence an octave up. Instead of

2.9

To compare to Figure 2.8, here are two tiers of the Training Spiral. You can see the repetition of the elements (represented by the different-colored bands) as you progress. ▲

2.10

Comparison of a musical scale repeated at different octaves with the sequence of elements repeated at a higher level. ▲

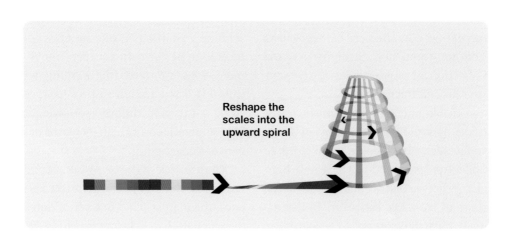

Reshape the scales into the upward spiral

starting our scales with the note C and ending on B above, we start with Rhythm and move up to Collection (fig. 2.10). When we repeat the sequence, it is with a higher degree of difficulty and quality, rather than a higher musical pitch.

Our Tower or "musical scale" can easily arrive at our Training Spiral structure—we simply take the Tower and bend it into a spiral shape (fig. 2.11).

★ When an Element Is Weak

When an element in a previous tier is not in place or is not working correctly, then the exercise the horse is being asked to perform in his current tier will likely fail. To illustrate the point, let's go back to our Tower representation and imagine an example. Suppose that one of the "bricks" (in this case, let's say it is the Impulsion brick in Tier 2) crumbles and falls apart (figs. 2.12 A & B). This means that the

2.11
Reshaping the sequence of elements to form the Spiral. ▲

two "bricks" above—Straightness and Collection—are now not secure and are likely to fall from the tower. The "bricks" (or elements) below the failed Impulsion are likely to remain unaffected. In other words, the horse cannot perform the degree of Straightness and Collection being asked at Tier 2, yet is still able to perform all the qualities of the elements up to the point of weakness.

How would this look in practice with a horse at Training Level?

Well, in this situation the horse may still be able to perform a lower-level movement, such as a 20-meter circle in

The element of Impulsion is failing at the second tier of the Tower (A). The elements above (Straightness and Collection) will therefore fail too (B). However, all the elements (and tiers) below the failed Impulsion may still be intact. ▼

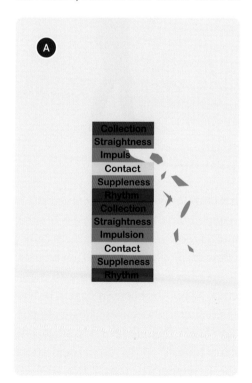

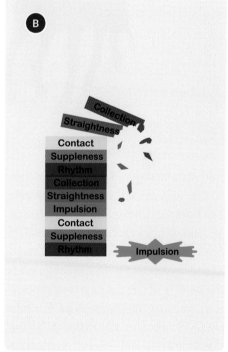

So, we can ride a pretty good 20-meter circle, now I want to try a 10-meter circle...

Oh, I don't have enough Impulsion to carry myself with that much bend!

Oh dear, it's all gone a bit wobbly.

Let's make it a little easier then and try a 15-meter circle. Then, as he builds more Impulsion, we can come back and try the 10-meter circle.

trot, and show a good degree of quality in all the elements of the Scales of Training. The rider then moves on to ride a 10-meter circle (a more challenging movement), finds that the horse is still maintaining a good rhythm on the 10-meter circle, and the quality of the contact is okay; however, because the horse does not have enough Impulsion, his ability to "shape" (Straightness) and "carry" (Collection)

his body onto the smaller curved shape required for a 10-meter circle is limited, and it is now very likely that the accuracy of the shape of the circle will not be good. If the rider moves back to the 20-meter circle again, the horse will again be able to produce a good-enough quality Impulsion (and other elements) to shape and carry himself on the curve required for the 20-meter circle (figs. 2.13 A & B).

2.13 A & B

In (A), the horse is being asked to perform a 10-meter circle, but as he doesn't have enough Impulsion, you can see him losing his straightness as his neck is beginning to bend too much. He is also falling onto his forehand, causing him to work in a more downhill manner. When the rider moves the horse back to the 20-meter circle in (B), he is able to maintain better quality on the size of circle with the amount of Impulsion he is currently working with.

end of chapter 2

The Training Spiral: The Scales of Training Remodeled

> *The Spiral can be applied over various time periods—from many years to a single training session.*

chapter

3

Timescales:
How Quick, How Long, and When to Go Back

3 ———————

As I've mentioned, the traditional Scales of Training imply that a horse's training starts with the lowest level, Rhythm, and reaches (or at least nears) completion when he reaches the top level, Collection. In the case of a dressage horse, this process can take eight years or more. There is nothing necessarily wrong with this structure or, indeed, this timescale. However, this very linear approach doesn't really help riders in their day-to-day, week-to-week, and month-to-month training. By contrast, the Training Spiral, when thought of as a conceptual model or framework, can be applicable over various timescales, ranging from a few minutes to several weeks, months, or even many years. The Training Spiral is also applicable to horses of *all* levels—not just those being trained to the highest levels.

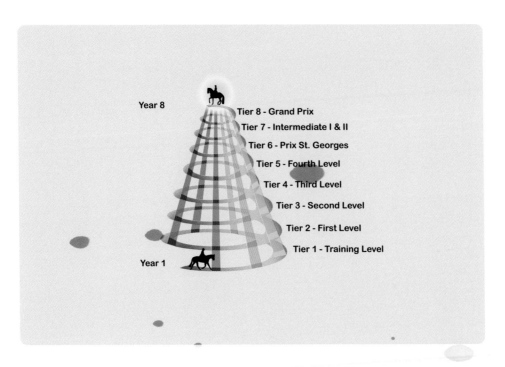

Year 8

Tier 8 - Grand Prix

Tier 7 - Intermediate I & II

Tier 6 - Prix St. Georges

Tier 5 - Fourth Level

Tier 4 - Third Level

Tier 3 - Second Level

Tier 2 - First Level

Tier 1 - Training Level

Year 1

3.1

The Training Spiral with the bottom tier representing Training Level and the very top tier representing Grand Prix Level, with tiers in between showing the progression through the other levels, each approximately covering a year of training. ▲

★ *Years, Months, Weeks, Minutes*

In general, the shorter the time period that each tier of the Spiral represents, the smaller the amount of development we would expect to obtain in each of the six elements before moving on to the next. In the examples that follow, I will show how the Spiral can be applied, not only over years (with each tier representing a year of training), but also over months (with each tier representing a month of training), or a period of weeks and even over a period of just a few minutes within a training session.

In previous chapters you saw how the Spiral can be applied to horses training

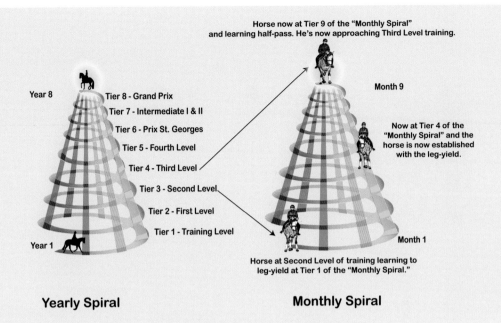

Horse now at Tier 9 of the "Monthly Spiral" and he's now approaching Third Level training.

Month 9

Now at Tier 4 of the "Monthly Spiral" and the horse is now established with the leg-yield.

Year 8

Tier 8 - Grand Prix

Tier 7 - Intermediate I & II

Tier 6 - Prix St. Georges

Tier 5 - Fourth Level

Tier 4 - Third Level

Tier 3 - Second Level

Tier 2 - First Level

Tier 1 - Training Level

Month 1

Year 1

Horse at Second Level of training learning to leg-yield at Tier 1 of the "Monthly Spiral."

Yearly Spiral

Monthly Spiral

from lower levels and progressing over years to more advanced levels. With time now in mind, consider again how the Spiral can be applied with a horse who is starting at Training Level and aiming to progress to Grand Prix (fig. 3.1). For this journey, one would be allowing for years of development, and each tier could represent each level of dressage training, roughly equating to a year per tier.

The Spiral framework can also be applied to the horse's month-to-month training (fig. 3.2). There is a similar progression upward from one tier to the next as you develop each of the six elements in turn. As each month passes, the horse improves each element and progresses

3.2

On the left we see the Yearly Spiral and on the right a sample of how the Spiral can be applied over a shorter time period of several months. In the Monthly Spiral, we are seeing a Tier 1 (first month) where the horse is already several years into his training (equivalent to Tier 3 or Second Level in the Yearly Spiral) and learning to leg-yield. After several more months of training, he will be at Tier 4 in the Monthly Spiral and well-established with the leg-yield, and several months after that he will be at Tier 9 of the Monthly Spiral and learning to perform a half-pass. At this point, he will be nearing Third Level in his training, thus will be approaching Tier 4 in his Yearly Spiral. ▲

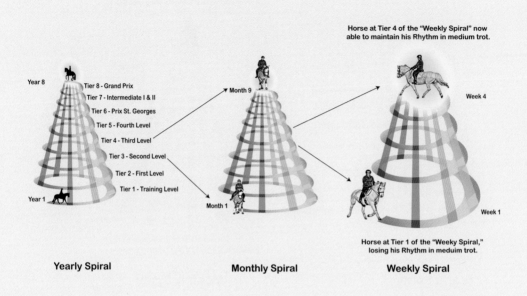

Horse at Tier 4 of the "Weekly Spiral" now able to maintain his Rhythm in medium trot.

Year 8

Tier 8 - Grand Prix
Tier 7 - Intermediate I & II
Tier 6 - Prix St. Georges
Tier 5 - Fourth Level
Tier 4 - Third Level
Tier 3 - Second Level
Tier 2 - First Level
Tier 1 - Training Level

Year 1

Month 9

Month 1

Week 4

Week 1

Horse at Tier 1 of the "Weeky Spiral," losing his Rhythm in meduim trot.

Yearly Spiral

Monthly Spiral

Weekly Spiral

3.3

On the left is an example of a Yearly Spiral, in the middle a Monthly Spiral, and on the right a representation of an even shorter time period: a Weekly Spiral. The Weekly Spiral shows a horse already at Second Level in his training and losing his Rhythm in medium trot in Tier 1 (week one); however, after a few weeks of training (Tier 4), he is able to maintain his Rhythm within his medium trot. This "snapshot" of training time would be found somewhere within the Monthly Spiral, which then fits within the Yearly Spiral. ▲

from one tier to the next. In this scenario, the degrees of improvement expected between one tier and the next are smaller than the improvements seen in the "Yearly Spiral" depicted in Figure 3.1 (p. 34).

For example, in the "Monthly Spiral" we may have a horse who is learning to leg-yield, and the improvement seen from one tier to the next (in this case, one month to the next) may just be that at the start of the month he loses his Suppleness and Impulsion toward the end of the movement, and by the end of the month he is maintaining a better degree of Suppleness and Impulsion through the *whole* movement.

In the Yearly Spiral the degree of improvement we might be aiming for from one tier (or year) to the next is from the horse being able to perform a leg-yield at Tier 3 (Second Level training) to the horse being able to perform a half-pass in Tier 4 (Third Level training). Comparatively, in the Monthly Spiral, the horse might be performing a leg-yield in Tier 4 (month four) and half-pass by Tier 9 (month nine), and all of that "fits" in the period of time it takes to move from Second to Third Level.

During your monthly training cycles, you may spend a week or so focusing on exercises that will improve Rhythm, followed by a week working on exercises to improve Suppleness, a week developing Contact, and so on, until you have been through all the elements of the Scales of Training, but as the degree of improvement expected for each element is smaller than in the Yearly Spiral, it all happens more quickly. This applies in a weekly training plan, too. Consider the horse working at Second Level who is inclined to lose his Rhythm when performing a medium trot; however, after a few more weeks of training (say, at Tier 4 of the "Weekly Spiral"), he is able to maintain his Rhythm during the medium trot (fig. 3.3).

In a Weekly Spiral, it may only take a day or two to complete improvement of each of the six elements, thus one tier of the Spiral may be completed in a week. Here, again, the degree of improvement

A FRAMEWORK ANYONE CAN USE

There are many books and there is a lot of literature on training exercises, how to perform them, and what they are aimed at helping, so in this book I don't go into those kinds of details. Instead, I provide the framework that can support and guide you as to where the focus of your training should be. Later chapters do provide some examples of how exercises can relate to the six elements and the Training Spiral at the different levels of training, as well as how these exercises can be progressively developed throughout the horse's training.

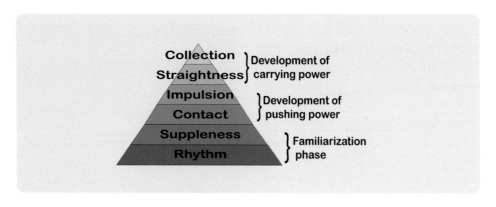

3.4

The three phases of training mapped onto the traditional Scales of Training pyramid structure. ▲

we are looking for in each element is even smaller still than what we expect with the Monthly Spiral. For example, as we saw in Figure 3.3 (p. 36), a horse working on his medium trot may be losing his Rhythm during the medium trot at the beginning of the week, but by the end of the week—once his Impulsion and Straightness have improved a little—he is the next tier up and his Rhythm has improved. After three or four weeks, he is able to maintain an improved Rhythm throughout his medium trot. It should be emphasized that the exercises ridden in Weekly and Monthly Spirals need not be specific to the improvement of each of the six elements of the Scales of Training. It is more that the trainer or rider shifts the *focus* of the exercises toward each element as the horse's training progresses through each tier. The Training Spiral is simply a conceptual framework, and the trainer has

to fill in the framework with appropriately selected exercises to suit not only the level of horse and rider but the elements they may be currently focusing on. If we look again at the horse who is losing his Rhythm in the medium trot (see p. 36), an exercise such as trotting poles would be useful in the maintenance of the Rhythm and raised poles could then be used to encourage more Impulsion.

★*Applying the Spiral in Day-to-Day Training*

As you can now see, there are a potentially infinite number of tiers within the Training Spiral, and the Spiral can also be applied over various time periods—from many years to a single training session. A rider may move up numerous tiers over a lifetime with a horse, with tiers representative of significant changes, or the rider may move up several tiers in one day, with each tier showing only very small developments in the elements over the previous tier. When the time period a tier applies to is only a few seconds or minutes, we are not expecting huge changes in the horses way of working— but they are progress.

At this point, it is useful to recall the three phases of training I described in chapter 1 (p. 6), since development of these three phases can be seen when training over days, weeks, months, and years (fig. 3.4). For example, if we consider a Grand Prix horse when he is at the very beginning of a Yearly Training Spiral (so, at Training Level), his degree of Pushing and Carrying Power will be minimal in comparison to when he is at the top of his Yearly Spiral eight years into his training after his strength is gradually developed during regular training sessions.

As with the six individual elements over the course of a horse's training, we need to follow a structure in which the three phases of training are repeated in turn: familiarization followed by development of Pushing Power, followed by development of Carrying Power... followed once again by familiarization, and so on (fig. 3.5). Again, the phases are not finite, as the traditional pyramid seems to suggest, but areas of development we seek to improve over and over again as new levels of understanding and physical conditioning are attained.

3.5

Now consider the phases of training mapped on to the Training Tower (p. 25 and left) and Spiral (right) frameworks. You can clearly see how the phases, like the six elements, are repeated as training progresses up each tier. ▼

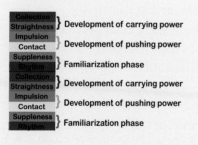

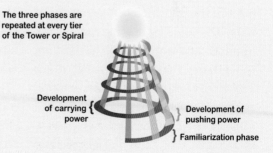

How Does All This Work in Practice?

Over the course of a single training session, for example, the horse may well progress up a tier and then lose an element (as you have already seen in the Tower structure—see p. 30), in which case the rider may drop back down a tier and re-establish the quality before progressing upward again. This may happen many times during one schooling session, emphasizing yet again the repetitive nature of the Training Spiral, even within a straightforward exercise lasting only five minutes or so.

To see how this works out in practice, let's take a quick look at Horace, a Third-Level horse, as he goes through the first stages of his daily session. As an initial warmup, he is allowed to have a stretch and a walk around the arena (Rhythm/relaxation and Suppleness—the *Familiarization Phase*). Next, the rider picks up a little more Contact and asks Horace to trot. They ride a few circles and practice the transition between trot and walk, before adding in some canter work (Contact and Impulsion—the *Pushing Power Phase*). The rider is now ready to ask a bit more of Horace and begins working on some leg-yielding (going sideways) and some more transitions between paces—for example, shortening and lengthening the trot (Straightness and Collection—the *Carrying Power Phase*).

Once he is warmed up, the rider can ask Horace to work some smaller circles and other movements around the arena—now with a working frame and a higher level of power (both *Pushing* and *Carrying Power*) within his trot (Rhythm/relaxation and Suppleness—the *Familiarization Phase*).

The rider works on more transitions and opens Horace's pace up into a medium or even extended trot, while maintaining the same quality within the rein contact (Contact and Impulsion—the *Pushing Power Phase*). They then work on some more lateral movements, such as the shoulder-in, which help to improve Horace's Straightness as well as his ability to sit and engage his hindquarters (Straightness and Collection—the *Carrying Power Phase*).

You can see from this little example how the rider has gone up a couple of tiers of the Spiral just within the warm-up section of a single training session. However, if you consider how the spiral could be applied within an even *shorter* timescale it will help you to think about how you use the different Scales of Training elements from one moment to the next. Let's look at a brief moment in time as the rider is trotting Horace around one lap of the arena:

Horace is a little lazy in his trot, so the rider applies more leg aid to ask for more of a working trot. That improves the trot; now the rider asks Horace to bend his neck to the inside, as he feels a bit tight in that area. Horace bends his neck and follows the rein, and this loosens his neck muscles so the rider can ask Horace to soften into the rein contact on both hands. Now the rider can ask for more energy from Horace, but it seems Horace has started to fall out through the shoulders so the rider positions him into a little shoulder-fore to help straighten him. That works, and he now feels lighter in his forehand, but after a few more steps, Horace has tightened in his neck again, and, as a result, the general quality of the trot and the contact is lost. In response, the rider drops the level of energy a little, and goes back to bending Horace's neck a bit to relax his muscles. A couple of steps later, the contact is soft again, and the rider can ask for the increased level of energy once more. This time, he maintains the straightness without the need for the shoulder-fore, and his trot becomes more uphill once again.

Can you spot the different Scales of Training elements that the rider worked through as they rode one lap of the arena? To help you, here is the same description again, but color-coded this time:

Horace is a little lazy in his trot, so the rider applies more leg to ask for more of a working trot. That improves the trot; now the rider asks him to bend his neck to the inside as he feels a bit tight in that area. **Horace bends his neck and follows the rein, and this loosens his neck muscles,** so the rider can ask Horace to soften into the rein contact on both hands. **Now the rider can ask for more energy from Horace,** but it seems **Horace has started to fall out through the shoulders, so the rider positions him into a little shoulder-fore to help straighten him.** That works, and he now feels **lighter**

★ COLOR KEY

RHYTHM
SUPPLENESS
CONTACT
IMPULSION
STRAIGHTNESS
COLLECTION

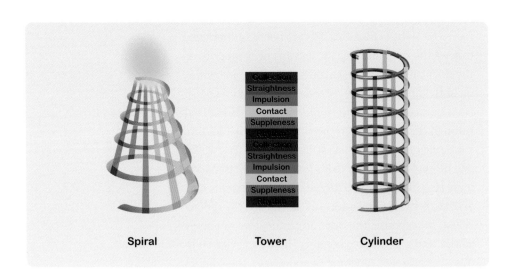

| Spiral | Tower | Cylinder |

The middle Tower labels (top to bottom):
Collection
Straightness
Impulsion
Contact
Suppleness
Rhythm
Collection
Straightness
Impulsion
Contact
Suppleness
Rhythm

in his forehand, but after a few more steps, Horace has tightened in his neck again, and as a result, the general quality of the trot and the contact is lost. In response, the rider drops the level of energy a bit and goes **back to bending Horace's neck a little to relax his muscles.** A couple of steps later, the contact is soft again, and the rider can ask for the increased level of energy once more. This time, he **maintains the straightness** without the need for the shoulder-fore, and his trot becomes **more uphill** once again.

Notice how the rider twice had to drop back and repair an element before progressing again. And remember—*all of this happened within one lap of the arena.* This example demonstrates how the Spiral concept can be applied over a very short period of time.

3.6

On the left is the Training Spiral framework, in the middle the Tower to which I have referred, and on the right, a possible cylinder shape. ▲

★ Why a Spiral, Rather Than a Cylinder?

It is true that since the Training Spiral is simply a conceptual framework, there is no reason why it could not be visualized

Tier 8 - Grand Prix
Tier 7 - Intermediate I & II
Tier 6 - Prix St. Georges
Tier 5 - Fourth Level
Tier 4 - Third Level
Tier 3 - Second Level
Tier 2 - First Level
Tier 1 - Training Level

"Yearly Spiral" where the long-term goal is to get from Training Level to Grand Prix

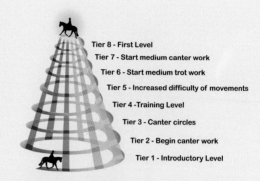

Tier 8 - First Level
Tier 7 - Start medium canter work
Tier 6 - Start medium trot work
Tier 5 - Increased difficulty of movements
Tier 4 - Training Level
Tier 3 - Canter circles
Tier 2 - Begin canter work
Tier 1 - Introductory Level

"Yearly Spiral" where the long-term goal is to get from Introductory Level to First Level

3.7

On the left is a Yearly Spiral for a horse starting at Training Level and aiming to progress to Grand Prix over a number of years. On the right is a Yearly Spiral for a horse that is starting at Introductory Level and aiming to progress to First Level, again over a number of years. Each example shows how at each tier (roughly equivalent to a year's training) the horse will progress to a new stage in his development. ▲

as a cylinder or spring shape—after all, we already used the alternative visualization of the Tower earlier in this book to demonstrate certain aspects of training (fig. 3.6).

No matter which visualization is used, the key thing about this concept is the progressive development of the horse by improving each element of the Scales of Training in order before proceeding, and repeating, the process at the next tier. However, the spiral shape is my preferred visualization for several reasons.

The main reason I veer away from basing a training framework on the cylinder shape is that it implies that the training process is endless...which of course it is!

But it is very important to have achievable goals for rider and horse to strive toward, and the spiral shape provides that. By using the Spiral over the different timescales of minutes, weeks, months, and years, we are provided achievable micro goals, short-term goals, medium-term goals, and long-term goals.

This principle of different goals applies not only to those aiming for Grand Prix but to the more novice riders whose long-term goals may be to get from Introductory Level to First Level with their horses (fig. 3.7).

There may be many reasons why a rider's long-term goal may not be

A horse with a weakness within the Suppleness element (represented by the orange vertical band) is likely to encounter this weakness at each level of the Spiral as he progresses through his training. ▲

Grand Prix. Not all riders have the hours available for training or have the resources that are required to achieve that high level. Many riders just want to develop themselves and their horses at a more leisurely pace. For others, their horses are also performing other jobs in life so cannot dedicate all their training time to dressage. The wonderful thing is that whatever riders' long-term goals may be, the Training Spiral can be used to help structure their training and thus help them achieve their aim.

★ Resurfacing Weaknesses

A horse often has a particular weakness that is seen to "resurface" at different stages of training. Maybe the horse struggles with Straightness despite progress in the other elements. Let's say he has a tendency to "go crooked," with his quarters in. At a lower level of training—for example, when working at First Level—this is identified and corrected. However, several months later, when his training is otherwise progressing well, the problem of his crooked hindquarters seems to reappear.

The rider may feel disappointed, as she may have thought she had already fixed this problem. The truth is that the problem *had* been fixed at First Level, but the horse then progressed up the Spiral and is now working with a more advanced degree of Rhythm, Suppleness, Contact, and Impulsion, causing his "weak area" to begin to show again within the more advanced level of work. If the rider were to drop back down to the previous tier of the Spiral and repeat the exercises she and her horse were working on a few months earlier, the horse would most likely lose his crookedness and go straighter again.

Do not, therefore, become too down-hearted when it seems as if you have to revisit an issue that you thought already "fixed." For one thing, this is simply part of the repetitive nature of horse training. For another, the re-emergence of the horse's weak element may very well be a good sign, indicating that he has progressed to a higher tier of the Training Spiral (fig. 3.8).

Conversely, some horses have a particularly strong element or elements, and during their training will often progress very quickly through these areas. For

example, a horse that has by nature an abundance of Impulsion is likely to require fewer exercises to help develop this element further, regardless of which tier of the Spiral he has reached.

Such resurfacing weaknesses can also be explained when we consider the phases of the training. One example is that you may find there are periods of time when the horse has developed greater Pushing Power than he has Carrying Power, and this can affect the quality of the Contact. The horse might become heavy in the rider's hand and use the Contact to balance; at the same time, as his energy is pushing forward, he becomes more powerful and thus stronger into the Contact. Riders can sometimes feel as if the quality of their horse's work has actually deteriorated; however, it is often simply that the horse has developed a greater level of "push" than he has strength to "carry."

★ GETTING PERSPECTIVE   🗨 rider 🗨 horse 🗨 coach

My horse gets heavy in the rein contact sometimes when I'm riding, but this is when he is developing his Pushing Power.

Sometimes I get so much power I can't contain it all and end up "running" forward.

There will be times when the horse has more Pushing Power, times when he has more Carrying Power, and times when you should just allow him to become comfortable and familiar with it all.

Since the horse has developed a greater degree of Pushing Power in this scenario, now, as part of his training progress, he needs to focus on the development of the Carrying Power elements—Straightness and Collection. If this is done with an appropriate amount of time allowed for the desired improvement, the horse should become lighter in the Contact again as all elements of that tier of training are put in place.

So, how would training on the Spiral progress from here?

The horse would then enter a new Familiarization Phase but working with his increased levels of power and Collection—that is, he would start the next tier on the Spiral. This training would be not so much about the introduction of new exercises but instead focus on the establishment of familiar exercises, now worked on with the new level of power and Collection the horse acquired during his time on the previous tier.

This "balance" between Carrying Power and Pushing Power is one that is repeated at every tier of the Spiral. Within a short time period, we often see very small shifts in this balance between carrying and pushing—a couple of simple transitions can often address the issue and find a better balance between the two. However, over a longer time period we may see a greater difference between the horse's ability to carry and his ability to push, as more time may be required for the horse to develop the muscle and strength he needs to adjust one or the other.

"Safety-Net Tier"

No matter at what stage the horse is in his training, it is worth having a "Safety-Net Tier." This is the highest tier at which the horse is well established and familiar with what is required. It is the tier that the rider may drop back down to should the horse become stressed or unsure about his work. Moreover, after you have introduced something new to a horse, it is always a good idea to spend a few minutes (or days, if necessary) back at the Safety-Net Tier; this is effectively the horse's "comfort zone," and it is wise to allow him some time there before asking the more challenging question again or asking a new question altogether.

Let's imagine a horse at First Level who has established a good quality of working trot and a good Contact. The rider then introduces the leg-yield, which the horse performs, but in doing so he loses the Contact. Moreover, when the rider tries to address Suppleness and Contact, the horse is still tense, and the rider cannot regain the quality they had before asking for the leg-yield.

This is a good example of when to go back to your Safety-Net Tier. In this case, the safety net may be found when the rider comes back to walk and asks the horse to stretch his neck longer, then picks up the rein and works a basic "1, 2, 1, 2" trot, without asking for a full "working" trot. Quite often, the safety net may be several tiers down the Spiral. But wherever it is found, it is important to have a comfort zone for the horse. If it takes more than a day or two for the horse to progress up the Spiral again with ease to the tier at which you were working, you should

★ GETTING PERSPECTIVE   💬 rider 💬 horse 💬 coach

Your horse is looking unsure and a little stressed about this new work.

That was a bit harder and now I'm not sure if I understand...

I agree. He feels a little anxious now.

Lets go back and do some work he is comfortable with for a few minutes.

Ah, okay! Everything is still the same, and I can relax again.

THE TRAINING SPIRAL | Sue Grice |

consider if you have perhaps pushed the horse too quickly to that tier. You may need to spend a little more time in the Familiarization Phase of the tier, before asking the horse a new question or increasing the challenge further.

Ideally, it will take no more than a few *minutes* to settle a horse at the Safety-Net Tier before you are able to progress once more.

★ *Key Points about Training Spiral Timescales*

- There is no exact number (in fact, there is a potentially infinite number) of Spiral tiers that can be carried out at any level of training.

- Some horses will naturally progress more quickly through some of the six elements and struggle with others.

- As long as progress is guided by the ability of both the horse and rider, that is the right speed of progress.

- Never be afraid or reluctant to drop back down a tier as and when needed.

- Remember the Training Spiral is only a concept or a guide to training and not a precise step-by-step instruction manual.

- Every trainer and every rider should apply the Spiral concept as they see fit for each individual horse, bearing in mind the stage of the horse's training and the rider's expertise.

end of chapter 3

Timescales: How Quick, How Long, and When to Go Back

It can take hundreds or even thousands of repetitions for a horse to truly know and understand a particular cue.

chapter

4

Communication and Choosing Priorities

4 _____

It should always be remembered that our communication with our horses is, in fact, quite limited. For example, a coach may say to a rider, "That transition you just rode was better, but you still need a bit more reaction to your leg aid," and without really thinking about it, the rider will take this to mean that what she just did was an improvement on previous attempts, but that there needs to be further improvement for it to be good enough. This might seem very obvious, but it is actually quite a complex idea, and one that riders would find impossible to convey to their horses. In fact, even the simple concept of "better" is pretty much impossible to communicate to a horse. The rider can only convey the idea that something was "good enough"– or that it was not. As training progresses, the level of what

▲ *The rider accepts what the horse has given her but is aware that it is still not totally correct.*

Both above and below examples are valid responses to the coach's remark, "That's better," but it is up to the rider to make the judgment call and let the horse know if what was offered was "good enough" or not.

★ **GETTING** PERSPECTIVE 🗨 rider 💭 horse 🗨 coach

▲ *Or, the rider does **not** accept what the horse has given her and insists on more.*

is acceptable can be raised and refined, so that "good enough" comes to mean something quite different as the horse's ability advances.

Bearing in mind the limited communication that is actually feasible, riders should keep signals to the horse clear and easy to understand. The way to do this is to make our communication as simple as possible.

Of course, as the horse's training progresses, the complexity of the movements and the "questions" being asked increases (see p. 59 where I talk more about how we use the word "questions" with horses). However, communication should still be built upon a basis of clear, simple signals.

Gadgets

This is a good point to discuss the use of "gadgets," such as stronger bits and additional pieces of tack, to achieve a desired result in the short term. Draw reins, for example, can be used to put the horse into a position where he *has* to work with his neck in a lower and rounder frame. The real question, however, is whether this helps the horse to understand what is being asked of him, or whether he is just being "put" into a particular position.

While there is a place for gadgets in training *when used properly by educated hands*, their use should always be carefully considered. Too often, such training aids can give the impression that the horse is performing well, when the reality is that the horse is simply being "held together" by the training aid and is not actually learning what the rider's signals or requests mean, or using his body in a healthy way. If the rider wants the horse to work correctly and be a willing partner, it is *essential* that at every stage of training the horse is given sufficient opportunity to learn and understand what is being asked, and how the rider wants him to respond to each particular question she asks. This means that the horse has to be able to interpret signals, such as a nudge from the rider's inside leg or a closing of the outside hand around the rein. The horse then has to react to these signals in the way the rider wants— in this case, bend more around the inside leg and slow down when the outside rein is closed. You might think these simple examples, but even the most basic of signals has to be learned by the horse. He is not born "just knowing" these things.

This means that it is absolutely vital to allow the horse the following:

- Time to learn.

- Sufficient opportunities to learn.

- Clear feedback to tell the horse whether his response is acceptable.

A rider will often introduce a new signal and, once the horse performs the correct movement or response a couple of times, assume that the horse has "got it." But the reality is that it can take hundreds or even thousands of repetitions for a horse to truly know and understand a particular cue.

This is not to say that the rider should condemn the horse when he provides an incorrect or inappropriate response to signals. Although the rider should be careful not to reward the incorrect response, she should recognize when the horse has *tried* to provide an answer to the question, even if it is not quite the correct one. In this situation, the feedback from the rider should be a quiet, "That's not quite right, let's try it again," type of response, which can be communicated by simply repeating the signal a little stronger. If, on the other hand, the horse's response is highly inappropriate, the rider's feedback could be a clearer, "No, not correct," such as the use of a stronger half-halt or stronger leg aid.

Whatever "correcting" feedback is used, it should not be so severe that the horse won't want to try again for fear of getting it wrong! Unless the horse is willing to try to find the answer for the rider, training will not progress in a happy and harmonious way.

When the horse's response is *correct*, again, clear feedback to the horse should be provided. This can be a verbal, "Good boy!" or a pat, or if the horse's response was really good then perhaps even stopping for a food reward (fig. 4.1). The level of positive feedback, like the "correcting feedback," should be proportionate to the effort and success of the horse's response.

Unfortunately, it seems to be human nature to notice the things that are *not* working (or are unacceptable), and when a horse provides an acceptable response, the rider quickly begins to just expect it and often does not provide any feedback. However, this approach can end up with the

4.1

The rider rewards her horse for trying hard to find the correct response to her signals.
The horse's happy expression shows that he is enjoying the positive feedback from the rider. ▲

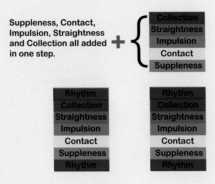

Suppleness, Contact, Impulsion, Straightness and Collection all added in one step.

+

Collection
Straightness
Impulsion
Contact
Suppleness

Rhythm
Collection
Straightness
Impulsion
Contact
Suppleness
Rhythm

Rhythm
Collection
Straightness
Impulsion
Contact
Suppleness
Rhythm

horse receiving more "correcting" feedback than positive "rewarding" feedback, which is not conducive to him being a happy and willing partner.

★ *The Need to Prioritize*

When working with the Training Spiral over a short timeframe (within a few minutes per Spiral, during a daily training session), we can think of our efforts to improve each of the six elements as if we are "asking our horse a question." For example, when we are working on Rhythm and the horse is going too fast, we will ask, "Can you slow down?" This would most likely be conveyed through a squeezing rein aid and perhaps through the seat. Another example could be if the horse was not straight and was working with too much inside neck bend, we might

4.2

The Training Tower being built with too many elements added to Tier 2 all at once instead of adding one element at a time. This can overwhelm the horse. ▲

▲ A rider's approach can affect her partnership with her horse.

▲ A better approach to training.

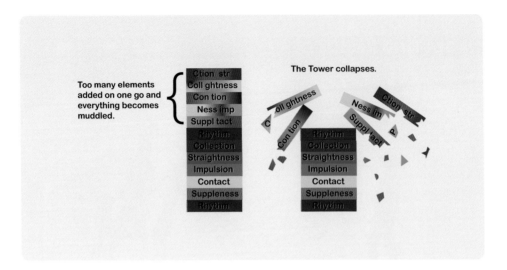

Too many elements added on one go and everything becomes muddled.

Ction str
Coll ghtness
Con tion
Ness imp
Suppl tact
Rhythm
Collection
Straightness
Impulsion
Contact
Suppleness
Rhythm

The Tower collapses.

Coll ghtness
Ness im
Ction str
Con tion
Suppl tact

Rhythm
Collection
Straightness
Impulsion
Contact
Suppleness
Rhythm

4.3

When too many elements are added at once, the elements that build the Tower become muddled, and the Tower collapses. ▲

ask, "Can you straighten your neck?" by applying more pressure on the outside rein. The important thing to remember is that *you should only add one element or ask one question of the horse at any one time.*

Often riders train their horses in a clear and well-structured manner, and the communication between the two seems to be working well. Yet as soon as they get to a competition, it all seems to fall apart. More often than not, the horse's puzzling lack of cooperation can be explained by the rider asking for everything all at once—*a failure to prioritize* causes a breakdown in communication.

Instead of asking the horse to progressively develop one element after the next as he moves along the tier of the Spiral (or Tower), as we have been discussing all the way through this book so far, what can happen is a rider tries to add too many elements (or ask too many questions) all at the same time (fig. 4.2). This is simply more information than the horse can take in at once.

When the rider attempts to add too many elements all at once (which in practice means asking too many questions at once), the communication between rider and horse becomes muddled and unclear. The result is most likely going to be that the Tower collapses, the horse becomes confused, and the expected improvement doesn't materialize (fig. 4.3).

At this point, it is common for both rider and horse to become frustrated. The rider becomes frustrated because the horse is not performing as well as she knows he can. The horse becomes frustrated because he does not understand what the rider is asking for—too many questions are being asked at once and he is confused (fig. 4.4).

4.4

Confusion leads to frustration between horse and rider. ▲

How to Prioritize

Since trying to communicate too many things at once (in other words, trying to develop too many of the six elements in any one moment) can lead to confusion, we need to decide how to prioritize what should be worked on at any given moment. An obvious starting point is the order of the elements as you ascend the Training Spiral:

- Priority 1: Rhythm

- Priority 2: Suppleness

- Priority 3: Contact

- Priority 4: Impulsion

- Priority 5: Straightness

- Priority 6: Collection

When you are happy with all of the six elements for the horse's stage of training, then you can move up a tier and begin the list again, with Rhythm as the first priority. For example, as the horse is warming up at the start of a training session, the degree of Suppleness that you expect won't be the same as when he is fully warmed up—that is, once he has gone through several tiers of the Spiral, say, 15 minutes later.

But, of course, training is not always so simple or straightforward. Although the Spiral provides a sound basic guide, things don't always go smoothly from one tier to the next.

We have already seen how it is often necessary to go back to a previous element, or even to go back an entire tier of the Spiral, in order to re-establish the quality in the horse's way of working. There is huge value in having that Safety-Net Level we talked about—a level that you can go back to when the horse becomes too confused or stressed in his training (p. 47). However, if the rider always takes

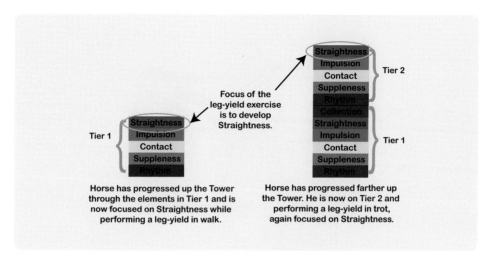

Focus of the leg-yield exercise is to develop Straightness.

Tier 1
Straightness
Impulsion
Contact
Suppleness
Rhythm

Tier 2
Straightness
Impulsion
Contact
Suppleness
Rhythm

Tier 1
Collection
Straightness
Impulsion
Contact
Suppleness
Rhythm

Horse has progressed up the Tower through the elements in Tier 1 and is now focused on Straightness while performing a leg-yield in walk.

Horse has progressed farther up the Tower. He is now on Tier 2 and performing a leg-yield in trot, again focused on Straightness.

4.5

On the left is Tier 1 of the Training Tower as the rider is asking her horse for a leg-yield in walk. The rider's focus for the exercise is on the Straightness element. On the right, the Tower has been developed to Tier 2, and the rider is now asking the horse to leg-yield in trot. Despite the change in gait that reflects the horse's development, the rider's focus is again on Straightness. ▲

a step back when something starts to fail or become muddled, she will never make any progress. The age-old saying about "learning from our mistakes" comes to mind. In life, sometimes we have to allow mistakes to happen in order to learn from them and go forward. The same is true when training a horse: on occasion you need to allow the horse to make mistakes in order to facilitate his learning.

This again raises the question of what to fix first. When something goes wrong, what should the rider ask the horse to do next? (Always bear in mind that you don't want to confuse the horse by asking too many things all at once and that in this assumed scenario, we are working within the context of the Spiral over a very short time period—within a few minutes, not a period of a week, month, or year.) The simple answer is that it depends on what the focus or aim of the training is *in that particular moment.* Do you remember Horace from chapter 3 (p. 41)? Let's now look at an example from when he was very young and just learning to leg-yield.

Horace had learned how to move sideways away from the rider's inside leg. On turning down the centerline, the rider applied her inside-leg aids to ask him to move sideways, and, when necessary, applied some slowing-down rein aids if he got too fast. This exercise really helped Horace develop a better degree

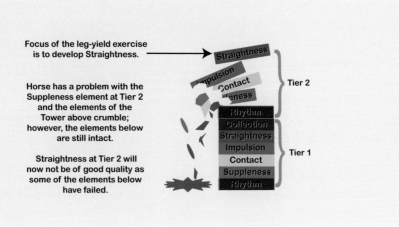

Focus of the leg-yield exercise is to develop Straightness.

Horse has a problem with the Suppleness element at Tier 2 and the elements of the Tower above crumble; however, the elements below are still intact.

Straightness at Tier 2 will now not be of good quality as some of the elements below have failed.

Straightness
Impulsion
Contact
Suppleness

Tier 2

Rhythm
Collection
Straightness
Impulsion
Contact
Suppleness
Rhythm

Tier 1

4.6

Due to a loss of Suppleness in Tier 2 of the Tower, not only is Suppleness in Tier 2 lost, but all the elements above it that have been developed so far—Contact, Impulsion, and Straightness—are also now being lost. Rhythm in Tier 2 may still be intact, and all the elements in Tier 1 may also still be okay. ▲

of Straightness through his body, and since it worked well in walk, the rider felt it was time to try it in trot. The purpose of performing this particular exercise at this particular time in Horace's training was to try and improve the Straightness within the trot (fig. 4.5).

Horace and his rider next trotted down the centerline and the rider applied her inside leg aids. Horace began to move sideways in a leg-yield, but he got a little braced in his neck and body. This meant that he lost some forwardness to the Contact and the trot lost its Impulsion. As Horace performed the leg-yield the Tower began to crumble (fig. 4.6). Since the Suppleness in his body was being lost, Horace was also losing the quality

within the Contact as well as some of his Impulsion.

At this point the rider had several options:

1. Stop asking for the leg-yield and ask Horace to soften in his body again.

2. Stop asking for the leg-yield and ask Horace to increase his Impulsion.

3. Stop asking for the leg-yield and ask Horace to move forward into the rein contact again.

4. Continue with the leg-yield and accept the lack of Suppleness, Impulsion, and Contact.

62 __

5. Continue with the leg-yield and ask Horace to improve his Suppleness, Impulsion, and Contact all at the same time.

The option the rider chooses will depend upon the aim or focus of the particular training exercise. In this case, the focus was to ask Horace to leg-yield in trot with the aim of improving his Straightness in trot. This being so, the applicable option here would be Number 4: Continue with the leg-yield and accept the lack of Suppleness, Impulsion, and Contact. At this stage in Horace's training he is not really well established with the leg-yield, and it is unlikely he will be able to perform the leg-yield perfectly—that is to say, maintain all the elements in Tier 2 during his leg-yield—so the rider should be willing to accept a loss of some quality in certain areas while Horace is improving his leg-yield in trot. In this case, despite the loss of quality in the Suppleness and the resulting consequences on the other elements above, the leg-yield Horace achieved *did* help improve his general Straightness.

What is really important when accepting a crumbling Tower like this is the amount of time the Tower's collapse encompasses. When learning a new exercise or movement, it may be expected that some loss of quality (a failure of some of the six elements) is inevitable; however, this loss of quality should only be very short-lived and a return to the desired quality (rebuilding of the Tower) should always be completed within a short timeframe of ideally seconds but not longer than a few minutes. The elements within the Tower (or Spiral) should always be "rebuilt" before the exercise is repeated again. In the example we've just illustrated with Horace, the rider should go back down her Spiral and work on improving the Suppleness, followed by the Contact, and then the Impulsion, to make sure these elements are all in place before re-attempting the leg-yield in trot. As Horace becomes more established with this exercise, he should be able to maintain the quality of the Suppleness, Contact, and Impulsion throughout the leg-yield.

If, however, the focus of the exercise is to improve Horace's Suppleness (rather than Straightness), the rider may choose a different option—perhaps Number 1: Stop asking for the leg-yield and ask Horace to soften in his body. In this case, the rider may choose to move onto a 20-meter circle and ride the leg-yield on the circle instead. This choice would help maintain and improve Horace's Suppleness as horses often find riding on the curve of a circle helps with their Suppleness, and it is easier to maintain this Suppleness through a leg-yield on the curved line rather than the straight line. Thus, the rider stops riding the leg-yield on the straight line but still accomplishes riding a leg-yield and maintaining the focus of the exercise: in this case, the Suppleness element.

So, as you can see, there is no definitive right or wrong answer to the question of what to prioritize. It very much depends upon what the focus or purpose of riding a particular exercise at a particular time might be. The only option that would *not* be a suitable choice in any situation would be Number 5: continue with the leg-yield and ask Horace to improve his Suppleness, Impulsion, and Contact *all at the same time.* Asking Horace to work on all these elements at once would just lead to unclear signals, confusion, and most likely, frustration in both rider and horse.

As this example makes clear, there are times when it may be acceptable for the horse to lose the quality in one or more of the elements when mastering a new exercise. However, once the new exercise has been performed, if any of the underpinning elements have been lost, the rider should return to her priority list to rebuild the quality to a suitable level for the horse's capabilities—that is, return to the Spiral and progressively develop each of the six elements, one at a time, in the correct order. This should be done *before* asking the horse to perform the unfamiliar exercise again.

It is important to emphasize that the acceptance by the rider of loss of quality in one or more elements *should only be for a brief moment in time,* and in general, the progressive principle of the Spiral should be adhered to. In other words, allowing some loss of quality only relates to the Spiral concept when applied over a *very short period.* When considering the Spiral concept over a longer time period of weeks, months, or years, then such a loss of quality in the elements should *not* be accepted.

If the horse struggles to re-establish the quality within each of the elements he had prior to an exercise, it may be useful to return to the Safety-Net Level (see p. 47). The rider should rebuild the horse's confidence and re-establish the quality within his work before challenging him with the exercise again.

Repeat Errors

Making mistakes is a perfectly normal part of training, and in most cases, a necessary condition for making progress. But what about those cases where the horse repeatedly makes the same error? In this situation, it may be necessary to take a hard look at the training and the questions the horse is being asked.

Firstly, the rider needs to consider if the horse is mentally and physically capable of performing the exercise. If the answer is clearly no, then there is little point in persevering with the training as planned. If, on the other hand, the horse is capable but continues to make the mistake, the rider needs to think about the feedback she is providing. It is quite likely that the horse has learned an incorrect response to the question, and thinks he is performing the exercise correctly when he is not. As always, communication is all. —

end of chapter 4

Communication and Choosing Priorities

> *Our journey to the 'top'*
> *or to our intended goal*
> *is unlikely to be a smooth progression.*

chapter

5

The Spirals Through the Levels

5 ——————————

Let's take a closer look at the Training Spiral and how it can be applied in practice. To get a clearer view, we will follow the progress of our friend Horace as we dip into some of his training sessions over a period of time. We will note precisely where he is on his "Yearly Spiral," as well as which element he is working on at each stage of his daily training as shown in the "Daily Spirals"—from Introductory Level right up to Grand Prix.

It should be noted that the Daily Spirals shown here are just visual representations of a daily training session and only show five tiers of the Spiral. Of course, in reality there would be many more tiers during a daily training session. The visual representation here assumes that the first tier is the warm-up period, Tier 3 is about halfway through a daily session, and the top tier is near the end of one.

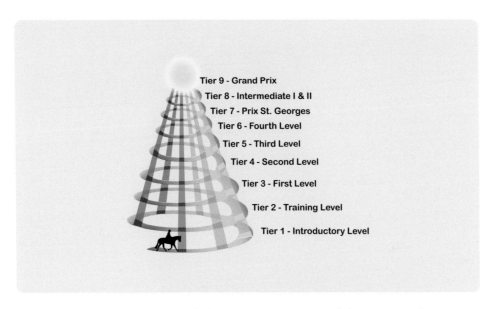

Tier 9 - Grand Prix
Tier 8 - Intermediate I & II
Tier 7 - Prix St. Georges
Tier 6 - Fourth Level
Tier 5 - Third Level
Tier 4 - Second Level
Tier 3 - First Level
Tier 2 - Training Level
Tier 1 - Introductory Level

★ *Training Horace at Introductory Level*

Our first visit to Horace is in the first few weeks of training at the very start of his Yearly Spiral (fig. 5.1).

During the warm-up in one of Horace's daily training sessions, his rider tries to establish some of the basics: The first element that she wants to establish is, of course, Rhythm (with Relaxation—see fig. 5.2). Unfortunately, Horace struggles to maintain a regular Rhythm, as he over-powers himself and goes too fast. When this happens, he breaks to canter in an attempt to rebalance himself. In other words, he is breaking from a two-beat Rhythm into a three-beat Rhythm and losing the correct Rhythm of trot. To help him, the rider tries slowing him down a little, and Horace finds it easier to maintain a trot without breaking to canter: for his stage of training (Introductory Level), he has now achieved a good degree of rhythm (1, 2, 1, 2, 1, 2) in the trot.

Next, how is his Suppleness? Can Horace bend his neck to the left and right, and when given a long rein (in walk), can he stretch down? The rider asks these questions of him,

5.1

A Yearly Spiral with Horace at the very start of his career at Introductory Level. The eventual aim for Horace is to become a Grand Prix horse. ▲

5.2

A Daily Spiral showing Horace working on Rhythm during the warm-up period. ▲

5.3

The Daily Spiral showing Horace as he moves on from Rhythm and works on Suppleness during the warm-up period. ▲

and Horace shows he can do as asked, although he finds it easier to flex his neck to the right than to the left. At Introductory Level we can accept this and be happy enough with his Suppleness (fig. 5.3).

What about his Contact? Really, all we need from Horace at this stage is for him to be happy to wear the bit in his mouth and to work *forward* toward the rider's hands without snatching at the reins or dropping the rein contact. The rider should be able to ask Horace to answer some basic aids, such as slowing down when pressure is applied to the reins (fig. 5.4).

Once the rider is happy that she has a degree of Rhythm, Suppleness, and Contact from Horace, she can apply her leg and ask him to put a little more energy (Impulsion) into his work (fig. 5.5). She does not want him to go any faster, so will need to use a little rein contact to contain this additional energy. This is why the quality of Contact needs to be in place first. Riding transitions at this point is useful when developing the additional Impulsion. Simple trot–walk–trot transitions are all that would be required at this stage.

If adding in more energy causes Horace to lose the Rhythm, or Suppleness, or quality of Contact that he had previously, the energy may have to be lowered so that these elements can be

5.4

The Daily Spiral showing Horace working on Contact during the warm-up period.

5.5

A Daily Spiral showing Horace working on Impulsion during the warm-up period of a training session. ▲

re-established (as we saw earlier on with the Tower example—see p. 62).

Assuming that Horace was able to add in the additional energy without losing the quality of anything else, the rider can start thinking about how to improve his Straightness (fig. 5.6). Most, if not all, horses are crooked—that is, not naturally straight. It is one of the aims of training to enable the horse to become more equal on each side. Now that Horace has enough Impulsion to support his body more, the rider can ask him to position his body into a better alignment. In Horace's case, there is a bit of a problem where he falls in through his left rib cage. The rider can

THE TRAINING SPIRAL | Sue Grice |

5.6

A Daily Spiral showing Horace working on
Straightness during the warm-up period
of a training session. ▲

5.7

A Daily Spiral with Horace showing an improved
degree of Collection during the warm-up period
of his training session. ▲

now begin to work on some exercises, such as a turn-on-the-forehand, which will help him to start to understand the concept of carrying his rib cage more to the right.

As a result of the work the rider has done with Horace, he has more energy, is beginning to carry a little more weight on his hindquarters, and his body is now a little bit straighter. In sum, he is carrying his body better—he has improved the degree of Collection he is working with (fig. 5.7).

This little example shows how even a horse at Introductory Level and only warming up can still work through each of the six elements of the Scales of Training. As his training session continues, he

moves up to the next tier on the Spiral and begins developing each element again, this time with a little more difficulty or higher degree of quality. For example, after his warm-up (on the next tier) Horace may be asked to develop his Rhythm, Suppleness, and so on while performing circles, therefore increasing the degree of difficulty very slightly. The degree of improvement from one tier to the next need only be very small. By the end of the session, the goal should be a small yet distinct improvement in the overall way he works (fig. 5.8).

In this case, by the end of the session, Horace is able to perform a figure eight

5.8

The Daily Spiral showing Horace now near the end of his training session, having worked through many tiers of the Spiral and showing the progression achieved for that day. ▲

in trot with a transition to walk over the centerline. He maintains good quality in his work while performing the exercise, so he has shown good improvement in this daily training.

★ *Training Horace at Third Level*

Now let's skip forward and drop in on one of Horace's training sessions a few years down the line (fig. 5.9). He is now working at Third Level, so his lateral work is well established; he can also show a good variation within the paces, with some collected and medium movements.

As at the earlier level, the rider will want firstly to ensure that his Rhythm is correct. When Horace was at Introductory Level (p. 68) this meant no more than trying to find a 1,2,1,2 Rhythm without breaking into canter; now, however, the rider is looking for a good quality *working* trot. That is to say, not just a trot trundling around the arena, but a trot that already has a good degree of Rhythm, Suppleness, Contact, Impulsion, Straightness, and Collection within it.

Now let's visit Horace halfway through one of his daily training sessions. He is already warmed up and has gone through several tiers of his Daily Spiral. Having established a basic level of Rhythm, Suppleness, Contact, Impulsion, Straightness, and Collection earlier in the session, Horace can begin working on

Tier 9 - Grand Prix

Tier 8 - Intermediate I & II

Tier 7 - Prix St. Georges

Tier 6 - Fourth Level

Tier 5 - Third Level

Tier 4 - Second Level

Tier 3 - First Level

Tier 2 - Training Level

Tier 1 - Introductory Level

Rhythm again, but at a higher level of quality and difficulty (fig. 5.10).

The rider will next want to check Horace's Suppleness within this level of trot. To do so, she may ask him, for example, to stretch forward and downward in the trot, or to leg-yield and move his rib cage over with ease in each direction. The degree of Suppleness asked for now is a little more than when he was at the bottom level of the Daily Spiral (when he was warming up—fig. 5.11).

The rider now expects a more secure Contact from Horace; he should be taking the Contact forward, as well as showing improved self-carriage (not resting his head on the rider's hands). When all this is working well, the rider can work on the Impulsion (fig. 5.12). At the tier Horace is now working, this could be achieved through exercises such as transitions within the gait, which allow the rider to "test" how well he can maintain the Rhythm, Suppleness, and Contact as she rides the transitions.

We know that when Horace was younger, he used to fall in through his left rib cage (see p. 70). This has improved a lot. In his warm-up during this training session, he

5.9

A Yearly Spiral with Horace at Third Level, Tier 5 of the Spiral, after several years of training. ▲

5.10

A Daily Spiral showing Horace working on Rhythm partway through his training session. He is showing good progression, but the aim of the session is to achieve yet more quality. ▲

5.11

A Daily Spiral showing Horace working on Suppleness part way through his training session. He is showing good progression, but the aim of the session is to achieve yet more quality. ▲

showed some nice leg-yield in each direction, and he is much straighter these days, as he has strengthened up and can now carry himself more evenly on each rein. However, he is still a little weaker on his left side—something that shows when he is asked to do the half-pass—as he doesn't maintain the same degree of bend on the left as on the right. This is something that he still needs to work on, so the rider does some exercises like shoulder-in, which help to improve his strength and bend a little more (fig. 5.13). Also, riding the shoulder-in helps Horace engage his

5.12

A Daily Spiral showing Horace working on
Impulsion part way through his training session.
He is showing good progression, but the aim
of the session is to achieve yet more quality
in all the elements. ▲

5.13

A Daily Spiral showing Horace working on
Straightness part way through his training
session. He is showing good progression,
but you can see that the aim of the session is to
achieve yet more quality in all six elements. ▲

hindquarters even more, and this helps
improve his ability to collect his trot.

There are perhaps two things above
all to note when studying this example
session with Horace. First, notice how the
rider still progresses through the six individual elements of the Scales of Training in order, although the starting point
(after warming up) is at a much higher
level than when he was young. Second,
Horace's "weakness" of falling in on the
left is still present, but it is now only
noticeable when he is asked to perform
a more difficult movement.

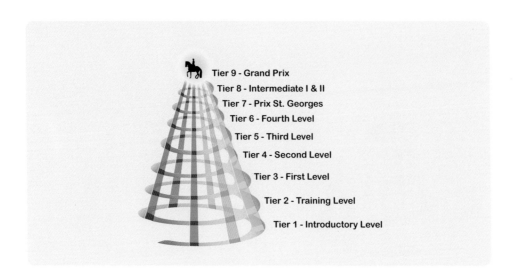

Tier 9 - Grand Prix
Tier 8 - Intermediate I & II
Tier 7 - Prix St. Georges
Tier 6 - Fourth Level
Tier 5 - Third Level
Tier 4 - Second Level
Tier 3 - First Level
Tier 2 - Training Level
Tier 1 - Introductory Level

★ *Training Horace at Grand-Prix Level*

Fast-forward several more years again, and Horace is now working at Grand-Prix Level (fig. 5.14).

Once again, let's take a quick look at one of his training sessions.

During the warm-up, the rider works Horace as if he were a Third Level horse—riding some variations within his gaits, varying his outline, stretching him long and low, as well as picking him up into a working frame. They ride some lateral work and gradually increase the difficulty of the movements and the degree of variation in the paces.

As the rider applies these exercises, she is still checking where his Rhythm, Suppleness, Contact, Impulsion, Straightness, and Collection are in terms of both quality and the degree of difficulty. This all happens over several tiers at the start of their Daily Spiral—they may perform some leg-yielding early in his training session to increase the Suppleness in Horace's body (fig. 5.15). If any one of the six elements are not up to standard as they progress, they will go back down the Spiral to a lower tier and work

5.14

A Yearly Spiral with Horace at Grand Prix, Tier 9 of the Spiral, after many years of training. ▲

5.15

A Daily Spiral showing Horace working
on his Suppleness during the warm-up period
of his training session. ▲

5.16

A Daily Spiral showing Horace working on
passage—a Grand Prix movement—after working
well through all the tiers of the session. ▲

on appropriate exercises to improve the problematic elements.

Let's say Horace is working well and the rider feels it is now time to try some of the Grand-Prix-Level movements. The rider asks for some passage (a highly elevated and very collected trot). Within this movement, Horace should still maintain a good quality in all the six elements (fig. 5.16). To start with, he keeps a very good Rhythm within the passage, but he becomes a little tight in the left side of his body. The rider responds by asking him to do a few steps of leg-yield within the passage to help to supple his body. This improves matters, but a few minutes later when they try the passage again, Horace loses the regularity of the Rhythm. The rider decides to drop down a couple of tiers of the Spiral and re-establish all the elements at a lower degree of difficulty—their Safety-Net Level (fig. 5.17). When she asks Horace to move back into the passage, she finds that his Rhythm is better again.

A little later in the session, the rider tries passage once again and Horace's Rhythm, Suppleness, and Contact are all good. At this point, she asks him for more Impulsion, and he produces an even more powerful passage, yet is now able to maintain his Rhythm along with all the other elements. He is now developing a top-level passage.

Note that although Horace is now working at the highest level, all the elements at the lower tiers of the Spiral are still required. They form part of his warm-up, and as he begins to work during a daily training session and is moved up the Spiral, the quality of each element is checked along the way. Even when he is consistently performing at the very top tier, it may sometimes be necessary to drop back down and "repair" certain elements before moving back up again.

In this chapter, you have seen simple examples of how the six elements of the Scales of Training can be applied at each level of a horse's training and at every stage of a training session. The Training Spiral gives a structure to enable progress within a session and a logical way of "fixing" things when they go wrong. In other words, the Spiral is a means of identifying what has gone wrong (which element failed) and how it might be fixed (dropping back down a tier or simply stepping back to a previous element on the same tier and reconfirming on that element). This goes against the traditional pyramidal understanding of the Scales, which implies, for example, that Collection is reserved for only the highest level of training.

The diagrams I've shared have shown how, within a daily training session, we of course only ask and expect a basic level from the horse during the warm-up period. Then, as he warms up, we can increase

5.17

When Horace loses his Rhythm in the passage, his rider drops back down a couple of tiers to their Safety-Net Level in order to re-establish the quality in all six elements. ▲

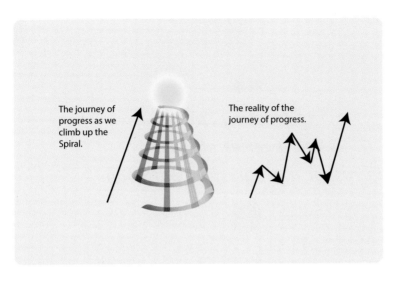

The journey of progress as we climb up the Spiral.

The reality of the journey of progress.

5.18

On the left we see how we would like our journey of progress to the top of our Training Spiral to proceed. On the right we see the reality of how our journey is likely to play out: moving upward, then taking a downturn before moving upward again. ▲

the challenge and expectation of quality. Toward the end of a training session, it would be hoped that the horse has climbed many tiers of the Spiral and is now working with even more quality through more complex movements. Of course, the journey to improvement is not always smooth, and the rider will often have to drop back down the tiers of the Spiral (fig. 5.18). Hence our journey to the "top" or to our intended goal is unlikely to be a smooth progression. —

end of chapter 5

The Spirals Through the Levels

"

The Training Spiral
is not a series of rules
but rather a progressive pathway.

"

chapter

6

Using Transitions

6 ——————————

There are many individual exercises that we can perform in training, and these can be used in several different ways, depending on the type of horse and the stage of training. Suffice it to say that the combinations of exercises are limitless. The aim of this book is not to provide lots of examples of such exercises, but rather to provide a concept that explains how any one exercise may be used in different ways for the different elements and levels of training.

In order to get a better understanding of this idea, let's look at how it applies to one type of exercise in particular: those involving the transitions between gaits and paces. Apart from anything else, I want to show how a rider can use these transitions to identify where she and her horse are in their training—and how to help develop the horse further.

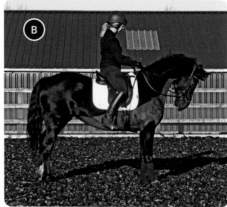

During this trot-to-walk transition, the horse in Photo (A) has tensed up and lost his relaxation, causing him to shorten his stride and jog from the trot to the walk. The young horse in Photo (B) has dropped from trot directly to halt when being asked to walk, which also causes a loss of the desired Rhythm in the walk. ▲

★ *Analyzing the Elements in Transitions*

To start, let's look at a simple trot-to-walk transition. This is something that almost all riders and horses can manage—the only exceptions being the most novice of riders and perhaps horses at the very start of their training career.

How can we judge the quality of a trot-to-walk transition using the elements of the Scales of Training? What are the questions to ask and the most common problems to arise?

Rhythm

Does the horse maintain a good clear Rhythm before and after the transition?

A good Rhythm makes the transition look and feel smooth and fluid, with the horse traveling forward in a relaxed way. The rhythm change (in this case, from the two beats of trot to the four beats of walk) should appear seamless.

Common Problems

The horse often goes from a trot to a walk, but then jogs a step or two before finally finding a clear walk beat (fig. 6.1 A). This can indicate a lack of relaxation. On the other hand, sometimes the horse will go from trot to halt before moving off into walk (fig. 6.1 B). This lack of relaxation and forwardness will result in a lack of Rhythm directly before or after the transition.

Suppleness

Does the Suppleness in the horse remain the same through the transition?

Ideally, the horse will be able to maintain the Suppleness in his muscles through the transition from one pace to the next.

6.2

As this horse is performing a trot-to-canter transition, you see how he loses his suppleness and becomes stiff over his back and his neck is raised up. ▲

Common Problems

The horse may tighten in his body as he performs the transition, which will present in his neck becoming stiff and raised up (fig. 6.2). Any kind of bracing from the horse is likely to cause the transition to become jerky or abrupt, although the Rhythm before and after may remain true.

Contact

Does the horse maintain a nice feel on the rein, taking the rider's hand gently forward? Does he respond to signals through the rein and body that prepare him for the transition? Does he stay forward, soft, and accepting throughout the transition?

Ideally, the horse should not get heavier or tighter, or block against the rein contact, when performing a transition. This applies likewise to the seat and leg aids that the rider applies.

6.3 A & B

The horse in Photo (A) is clearly taking hold of the reins and diving through the contact to the extent that the reins have even pulled the rider forward out of the saddle. In contrast, the horse in Photo (B) has dropped the rein contact and is not taking the rider's hand forward at all. ▲

Common Problems

The horse may take hold of the rein contact or block against it and push forward (or dive) through it (fig. 6.3 A). Alternatively, he may drop the rein contact by becoming too light on the rein and not taking the rider's hand forward enough (fig. 6.3 B). There are several reasons why a horse may do these things, but one surprisingly common cause is that he does not fully understand the question that the reins are asking; as a result, he tries either to avoid the contact or to take charge of it.

Impulsion

Does the horse maintain a good level of Impulsion (energy) before, during, and after the transition?

Ideally, the level of energy should not increase or decrease through a transition. Remember, walk is not necessarily a lower-energy gait than trot. It is just a different beat—that is, the legs are working in a different sequence and Rhythm.

Common Problems

One of the most common problems when going from trot to walk is that the level of energy or Impulsion can decrease. As a result, the horse, who may have had a good quality, active trot, moves into a walk that is lacking energy. Although the Rhythm may be a clear four beats, and the Suppleness and Contact remain good, the walk itself may be considered lazy, and the rider has to work hard to maintain the walk rather than the horse showing a desire to move forward.

Straightness

When riding a transition on a straight line, such as the centerline, does the horse stay straight and travel on two tracks?

Ideally, the horse will maintain the alignment (Straightness) through his body when performing a transition.

Common Problems

It is not uncommon for a horse to lose Straightness when performing a transition, perhaps most typically by falling out through his outside shoulder (fig. 6.4). However, some horses have a tendency to move always through the right or the left shoulder, whether this is the inside or outside one.

Collection

Does the horse feel as though he maintains a lightness and balance in his body as he performs the transition?

Ideally, the horse will maintain, or even increase, the degree of "sitting" power (Collection) he already has from the trot through to the walk.

6.4

While riding a trot-to-walk transition, this horse loses his Straightness
and falls through his right shoulder. ▲

Common Problems

In a downward transition (for example, from trot to walk) a horse can often lose the Collection, which can be identified by the horse "diving onto the forehand." In other words, his body weight shifts from his hindquarters onto his shoulders, and he becomes downhill in his way of moving (fig. 6.5).

As the horse works with the more advanced levels of Collection, it is easy for him to get "stuck" in the collected pace and lose the forward desire. This can occur when the horse begins to carry too much weight with his hindquarters and doesn't have enough forward impulsion—he "bounces" up and down with little or no forward inclination. Once again, when you find problems occurring at the

6.5

Here you can see the horse has lost his collection and is falling downhill onto his shoulders during a canter-to-walk transition. ▲

highest level of training, the issue is most easily fixed by returning to a lower tier of the Spiral and progressing upward once more.

When riding a transition, the six elements (Rhythm, Suppleness, Contact, Impulsion, Straightness, and Collection) can be identified by any level of rider at any level of training (it is part of a rider's training to become increasingly aware of them). The difference between novice and advanced levels lies in the degree of quality and precision that is being asked for and is expected from the horse. For example, a rider at Introductory Level may need to use an increased amount of rein contact to ask the horse to perform a transition from trot to walk, whereas a Grand Prix rider may rely almost entirely on subtle seat aids. Similarly, at Introductory Level it is satisfactory for a horse to move from trot into a walk that has a clear four beats but is lacking a little in energy. As long as the horse is still moving forward in walk, it may be acceptable. However, at the more advanced levels a rider would not be satisfied with a "lazy" walk and would require a much higher degree of Impulsion from the horse since he may be required to perform an advanced movement from the walk.

There is no precise rule as to what is acceptable or not acceptable at each level, as training should always be tailored to the individual rider and horse. The Training Spiral is not a series of rules but rather a progressive pathway that a rider or coach can take when training a horse. Knowing exactly where one is on that path, and how big a step to take next, is part of the art of training.

★ Transition Exercises

To get a better idea of how this works, let's look at some of the various transition exercises that can be carried out at the different levels of training for each specific element.

Although at this point we are focusing solely on transition exercises, the same concept can be applied to many other exercises (for example, leg-yield, circles, serpentines, shoulder-in) where the difficulty and the quality required from the horse are tailored to the stage of training.

Rhythm

At all levels of training the aim is the maintenance of a good clear Rhythm both prior to and after the transition so there is a seamless change of pace or gait without any stuttering or jogging steps. To achieve this, the rider must develop a good feeling for the horse's Rhythm and the ability to adjust it when required by using signals the horse clearly understands.

The horse also needs to feel happy and confident about the questions being asked of him in order to maintain a relaxed, yet forward-thinking, Rhythm throughout the transitions. Even in the downward transitions, you want the horse to be forward-thinking—after all, the horse should still be traveling in a forward direction when going from, say, trot to walk. What follows are three sample levels of training and the transitions that might be expected.

6.6

This horse is showing good Rhythm and relaxation in his walk following a downward transition from trot to walk. ▲

First Level

We have already looked at the basic transition from trot to walk, but there are, of course, many other transitions that can be ridden at this level, including:

- Walk – Trot
- Trot – Walk
- Trot – Canter
- Canter – Trot
- Walk – Halt
- Halt – Walk

The same principle of the maintenance of Rhythm prior to and after the transition applies not only to the trot-to-walk transition (fig. 6.6) but to *all* transitions, even the halt, as the horse should hold an immobile position. Often horses will drift or fidget by taking one or two small steps in the halt, which one could regard as a lack of Rhythm.

Third Level

At this level the degree of difficulty is increased although the basic aim is still to achieve a good quality of Rhythm throughout. Transitions at this level may now include direct transitions (transitions that "miss" out a gait) such as:

- Trot – Halt
- Halt – Trot

6.7

Here, the horse has been asked to come from a medium canter into a collected canter during a dressage test. He is maintaining a good canter Rhythm as he moves from the medium into the collected canter, and now shows more of the Carrying Power that is required in the collected canter. ▲

- Walk – Canter
- Canter – Walk

The horse will also be expected to show transitions within the gait, such as a transition into collected canter from a medium canter (fig. 6.7). Other transitions within the gait that can be performed at this level include:

- Collected Trot – Medium Trot
- Medium Trot – Collected Trot
- Collected Canter – Medium Canter
- Medium Canter – Collected Canter

Fourth Level

By this stage, the transitions introduced at First Level should be very well established; the Third-Level transitions might be used as part of the warm-up before the rider starts to ask for even more challenging transitions. The aim of maintaining a good Rhythm will be unchanged, but the difficulty of the transitions will once more be increased, depending upon how advanced the horse is (fig. 6.8). Transitions at Fourth Level may now include:

- Canter – Halt
- Halt – Collected Trot
- Collected Trot – Extended Trot
- Extended Canter – Collected Canter

6.8

The same horse we saw in Figure 6.7, now working at a higher level (here, Prix St. Georges), showing a good quality square and immobile halt. ▲

Suppleness

Assessing, maintaining, and developing the horse's Suppleness throughout the transitions is an important part of his training at all levels. The focus here is on the horse maintaining his ability to stretch and flex his muscles while performing the transition. Of course, in order to perform any transition, the horse will need to have a degree of "relaxed tension" (or "positive tension") in his body to carry him from one gait or pace to the next. As with Rhythm, the difficulty of the transitions is increased at each level of training—let's again just look at First, Third, and Fourth Level as examples.

First Level

Can the horse follow the rider's rein when it asks him to bend his neck? The point

6.9

Here the horse is working into a longer and lower frame by lowering his head and neck, while still maintaining good rhythm and activity in his hind legs. ▲

THE TRAINING SPIRAL | Sue Grice |

6.10 A & B

In Photo (A), you see a horse warming up for his dressage test being asked to move from a collected trot into a working trot while executing a half-pass. The engagement of the hind leg is clear to see. Photo (B) shows another horse in training performing the same exercise of transitions within the gait while performing a half-pass, but seen from a different angle. You can see a good degree of Suppleness from the horse in this image. ▲

here is not to bend the horse's neck for the sake of it, but rather to make sure that he maintains the *ability* to move his neck. It's about gently bending and straightening the horse's neck to check his flexibility, rather than making him bend.

Can the horse maintain the same degree of suppleness in his neck before, during, and after the transition is performed? This is a way of checking the horse's lateral Suppleness though his neck.

Can the horse perform basic transitions, such as walk – trot – walk, on a slightly longer, lower frame? This is tested by working the horse on a longer rein, but with the horse still maintaining a forward Contact. This exercise checks the horse's Suppleness over the top of his back.

Third Level

Can the horse perform transitions in a long, low outline? This is similar to the exercise just described, but with the degree of long and low increased (fig. 6.9).

Can the horse perform basic transitions while leg-yielding? This will check the lateral Suppleness in his body during a transition.

Fourth Level

At this level, you can ask the horse to perform transitions such as collected trot – working trot within lateral movements like shoulder-in or half-pass (figs. 6.10 A & B). Again, these exercises check the degree of lateral Suppleness, but at a much higher level.

Contact

Having the horse soft and accepting of the Contact yet still forward to the rein is the key here (fig. 6.11). It is also important to develop the horse's responsiveness to the rider's seat, leg, and rein aids, so that smaller and smaller signals can be given. Let's look at examples at two levels of training.

First Level

Here are two examples of transition exercises that are particularly useful for developing the horse's responsiveness to, and acceptance of, the aids.

- **Quick Transitions** – This involves riding several transitions in quick succession, for example: walk four steps – trot two steps – walk four steps – trot two steps.

6.11

This horse has a lovely forward yet soft contact on the reins as he performs his trot to canter transition. ▲

- **Half Transitions** – The rider prepares the horse to perform a transition, but then "changes her mind" before actually executing it. For example, starting in trot, the rider prepares to walk, but then continues in trot.

Fourth Level

The same exercises can be performed at Fourth Level but with a greater degree of difficulty. At Fourth Level, for example, the difficulty of the quick transitions could be increased by riding the walk for four steps – canter four steps – walk four steps, and so on.

Similarly, the half transitions could be developed further by using more seat and fewer rein aids in the preparation for a transition that *doesn't*, in fact, come. The subtlety of the exercise can also be increased by refining the half transition into a quarter transition (going a quarter of the way to walk before the

6.12

Here, the rider is giving an "invisible" half-halt signal to the horse to prepare him for the next movement coming up in the test. ▲

"change of mind"), and then a one-eighth transition. Eventually, what you are left with is a miniature preparation that the horse and rider are aware of, and reacting to, but is invisible to anyone watching. In essence, it has become a very subtle half-halt. Half-halts are a part of everyday riding and can be used when preparing a horse for the next movement (fig. 6.12).

Impulsion

The key to increasing Impulsion through the various transitions is to maintain the activity of the horse's hind legs and to make sure the energy continues to travel from the hind legs, forward through his back and neck, and into the rider's hands (fig. 6.13).

Do you notice a link here between Impulsion and Contact? In order to further

6.13
You can clearly see how this horse is pushing very well with his hind legs into this trot transition; however, there is little evidence in this particular photograph to suggest he is also producing Carrying Power—that is, upward elevation. In addition, the rider could allow the horse to go more forward in the rein contact. ▲

improve the forward feel of the Contact, a horse will need an increased amount of Impulsion—another tier on the Spiral.

First Level

A good exercise at this level is for the rider to look carefully at what the horse does with his legs when performing an upward transition (for example, walk to trot). Does the horse "pull" himself into trot with his front legs, or does he "push" with his hind legs? If he is pulling with his front legs, he is not working with Impulsion. The rider should ask the horse to become more active and quickly step into trot with his hind legs. At the same time, she can gently contain the horse's desire to pull himself into trot with his front legs by asking him to wait a moment longer in walk, using the rein contact. In basic terms, this means asking the horse to wait while "revving up" the hindquarters. This should result in the horse stepping into trot with an active hind leg, thus developing an increase in his Impulsion.

Third Level

The same goal of getting the hind legs to become more active through the transitions should be pursued at this level, but in the downward transitions as well as the upward. So, for example, in a trot – walk transition, the rider might ask the horse to maintain the active steps in the hind legs for a moment longer than would be required for a "dressage-test-quality" transition. This kind of training encourages the horse to develop a more active hind leg through all his transitions, both upward and downward.

It should be noted here that when these particular transition exercises are first introduced, the horse may lose some of the quality of the Rhythm. This is acceptable as long as the rider can return to the basic transitions and re-establish a good Rhythm relatively quickly (the Safety Net Level—see p. 47). As the training progresses up the Spiral, the horse should be able to perform these exercises while also maintaining his Rhythm.

Fourth Level

Impulsion can be developed further by ensuring that the horse maintains the activity of his hind leg when performing transitions within a gait (fig. 6.14). The same is true when riding downward transitions—for example, when riding extended trot to collected trot, the horse should not become lazy or slow in the hind leg. On the contrary, he should maintain the hind-leg activity and the push through his body even though the rider has asked

6.14

This horse has just performed a transition into a medium trot with good Impulsion. You can also see how he has a clear moment of suspension—that is, elevation off the ground—because at this level, he has developed good Carrying Power as well as Pushing Power (see p. 6). ▼

him to shorten the length of the step in his trot.

As already explained, horses can perform the same or similar movements but with varying degrees of quality, depending upon where they are on the Training Spiral. We can see an example of this is if we compare Figure 6.15 to Figure 6.14. The horse in Figure 6.15 is performing a very nice medium trot; however, he does not yet show the expression, power, uphill movement, or elevation that the more advanced horse in Figure 6.14 is able to show.

6.15

Like the horse in Figure 6.14, this horse is executing a medium trot, but while he has a good rhythm and ground cover, you can see he has not yet developed the strength in his hindquarters required to produce the amount of "lift" or Carrying Power the horse in Figure 6.14 is able to produce. This horse is working well but is still at a lower tier on the Training Spiral. ▲

6.16 A–C

At First Level, we may accept the level of Straightness shown in Photo (A). The horse is not totally straight as he is falling a little through his left shoulder. At the more advanced level of training seen in Photo (B), we would not accept the lack of Straightness: The horse is falling slightly to the left and you can see the rider attempting to correct him. In Photo (C) he is straighter and at an acceptable degree of Straightness for where the horse's training level is at the moment. ▲

Straightness

Maintaining Straightness—the alignment of the horse's body—is very important when riding transitions. When the horse is crooked (falling or pushing either in or out through his shoulders, rib cage, or hindquarters), the Impulsion that has been developed at earlier stages will not be able to travel properly though the horse's body. The Impulsion will "spill" out the side somewhere, rather than being pushed forward from the horse's hind legs through his back and neck into the rider's rein Contact.

All Levels

At all levels, one of the best ways to assess a horse's Straightness through transitions is simply to ride straight down the centerline of the arena and perform a transition. The rider can then assess if the horse drifted or fell a little to one side or another during this exercise.

Again, it will depend upon the horse's level of training as to what degree of Straightness will be acceptable to the rider (figs. 6.16 A–C). With the more novice horse, a little "wobble" here or there is to be expected, but as the horse's training progresses, the rider should gradually become more critical of the degree of Straightness he maintains.

Even with a Fourth Level horse, riding a transition as simple as halt – walk on the centerline may highlight any small Straightness issues that exist. For advanced horses, the challenge may be increased by including transitions such as walk – canter.

A useful variation on this exercise is to ride walk, trot, and canter transitions on a circle. The rider needs to look out for any increase or decrease in the size of the circle and notice if the horse becomes crooked (loses his body alignment) during the transition. However, the halt transition should *not* be used when training a dressage horse on a circle, as this is not conducive to obtaining a square halt.

Once you have identified any Straightness issues, there are numerous exercises that can be used to improve the horse's alignment. These include leg-yielding during the transition if the horse is falling-in through the rib cage or leaning on his inside shoulder or the inside rein. Another useful exercise is riding transitions between two poles to help the horse maintain his Straightness (figs. 6.17 A & B).

6.17 A & B

We use two ground poles to help the horse in Photo (A), who is training at First Level, stay straight while riding his walk to trot transitions. The poles are also used to help maintain the Straightness of a more advanced horse in Photo (B) while he performs a canter – walk transition. ▲

6.18

This advanced horse is working on the transitions between collected trot and passage. You can see how he is engaging his hind leg more, and this provides the "lift" in the trot that will be developed to eventually give the passage its expression. Note the horse could be taking the rein contact more forward; in this moment he appears slightly behind where we'd like him on the vertical. ▲

6.19

This horse is being asked to collect the canter steps in preparation for riding a canter pirouette. Note how the horse is carrying more of his weight with his hindquarters. Notice also how light he is in the rider's Contact. In this case, it is because of an increase in self-carriage rather than dropping the rider's hand. ▲

Collection

As with the previous elements of the Scales of Training, various levels of Collection can be seen at the various tiers on the Spiral. Unlike the other elements, however, Collection is not something that one attains by riding special exercises geared to achieving just this single quality. Rather, Collection is an expression of all the previous elements working together in harmony, the outward sign of which is an increased ability of the horse to carry his body in an uphill way.

Instead of giving specific exercises to develop Collection, I will suggest various ways of identifying this quality through transitions at several different sample levels. I would just add that, in order to develop collection, you should aim to improve Rhythm, Suppleness, Contact,

Impulsion, and Straightness, and from improvements in all of these, an improvement in the horse's ability to collect will become evident.

First Level

When riding a transition does the horse maintain the same weight on the rein Contact? Does his body have the same feeling that it is traveling uphill before, during, and after the transition?

Third Level

At this level, the rider can increase the difficulty to include more demanding transitions, such as canter – walk. The more collected the canter, the easier the horse will find it to step forward into walk while still maintaining his uphill body position.

Transitions within the gaits can also be included here, in particular, the transitions to medium and collected paces. Ideally, the horse should be able to maintain his uphill Carrying Power through all these transitions, but again, if it falls apart, it is the earlier elements that should be addressed.

Grand Prix Level

For the very advanced horse, the passage and piaffe transitions can also be included, as can the transition from a collected canter into an extreme collected canter in preparation for the canter pirouettes, or from the extreme collected canter out to a collected canter (figs. 6.18 and 6.19).

end of chapter 6

Using Transitions

chapter

7

Exercise Development —The Progressive Vision

7 ——————— IN this chapter, we will look at how individual exercises can be developed from a very basic foundation up to the Grand Prix Level. The emphasis here is not on showing you 101 exercises that can be used in your training sessions, nor is it about providing a detailed explanation of how to train or ride each of these exercises. Rather, the aim is to show how you can gradually increase the difficulty of any given exercise in order to advance your horse's training in a progressive way.

There are, of course, many different exercises and combinations of exercises that can be used for this purpose, and which of these are most appropriate will depend upon the horse's strengths and weaknesses as well as his level of training. More specifically, it will also depend on what qualities the rider is aiming to develop in the horse at any particular time.

To benefit from the Training Spiral, riders should always be looking beyond their current level and toward the next steps in their own and their horse's training. Only by doing so, will they come to a full understanding of the level at which they are currently working and how it provides a foundation for future progress. Without a clear vision of how to proceed up the Spiral, there is a danger of stagnation at any point.

In my work, I often meet riders who have put "limits" on themselves and their horses, believing that they are only capable of progress up to a certain level. Ironically, this self-limiting is the one thing that prevents them from progressing further. What they need is a good coach who does not reinforce these supposed limits, but instead provides a clear, concrete vision of how to progress. Each progression, no matter how small, will take the rider and her horse further up the Training Spiral and prepare the way for the next advance. With time and effort, there really are no limits.

That said, nothing is more important than the welfare of the horse and we should always bear in mind the physical and mental strain we put on him when asking for a higher level of performance. This does not mean that a "non-conventional" dressage horse—such as a Traditional Gypsy Cob or a Quarter Horse, for example—is incapable of performing high-level dressage movements, such as canter pirouettes or piaffe. Far from it! But if his conformation is not conducive to these types of movement, you should take care not to over-ask the horse. It may be a much harder exercise for him than for a horse bred specifically for the job. Likewise, if you are considering a show jumper, there may well be limits as to how high a particular horse can jump, even with the very best training.

★ Progressive Exercise 1 – From Circle to Serpentine

For our first example, let's look at how you can develop a very simple movement, the 20-meter circle, into a very advanced movement—the five-looped serpentine in canter with a flying change each time the horse crosses the centerline (figs. 7.1 and 7.2).

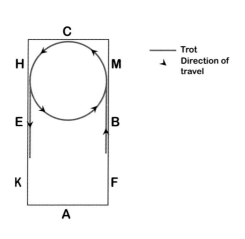

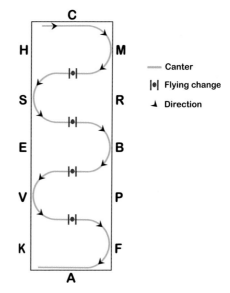

——— Trot
⊿ Direction of travel

——— Canter
|•| Flying change
⊿ Direction

7.1

The 20-meter circle at C ridden in a 20-meter by 40-meter arena. ▲

7.2

A five-looped serpentine in canter with a flying change each time the horse crosses the centerline, ridden in a 20-meter by 60-meter arena. ▲

Here the more advanced horse may well start his session with the basic 20-meter circle as part of his warm-up, then go through each of the stages described in the pages that follow before performing the five-looped serpentine. The younger or less experienced horse, however, may only achieve the first two or three movements I explain within one session, and it may take years of training before he is able to complete the most advanced stage. The key is applying the concept of the progressive nature of the Training Spiral,

but over an appropriate timescale that suits the horse's stage of training—and the rider's stage of training too.

Whatever the level, start by riding the simple 20-meter circle and checking that the horse is able to maintain all the elements of Rhythm, Suppleness, and Contact (and so on) while doing so (fig. 7.3). For a very novice horse, this, in itself, might be enough of a challenge.

Once the horse is confident and able to complete the 20-meter circle in each direction, you could link two circles together to form a figure-eight exercise (figs. 7.4 A & B). Now the horse has the added difficulty of having to change the bend and the direction of travel. Various things can go wrong—for example, the horse can lose his balance if he changes direction before

7.3

A horse on a 20-meter circle with a visualization of the circle superimposed to demonstrate the path the horse will take. ▲

B

A figure eight (A) and how it can be ridden
in the context of an arena (B). ▲

A ———————————————

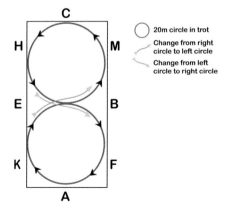

C

H ⬤ M

○ 20m circle in trot

⤸ Change from right
circle to left circle

⤸ Change from left
circle to right circle

E ⬤ B

K ⬤ F

A

reshaping his body onto the new bend.
In other words, he loses his Straightness
or alignment with the direction of bend
required. So, as with the 20-meter circle,
this can be challenging enough for a very
inexperienced horse or can be a very good
warm-up or suppling exercise for a more
advanced horse.

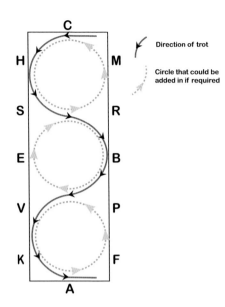

Direction of trot

Circle that could be
added in if required

7.5

Three-looped serpentine ridden in a 20-meter
by 60-meter arena showing how 20-meter circles
can be added into the serpentine if needed. ▲

As the horse's training progresses and he shows that he can maintain a good quality throughout the movements, the difficulty can be increased by developing the exercise as follows:

Three-Looped Serpentines

These can include a circle within each loop, to allow the horse more time to establish the quality before moving on to the next change of direction (fig. 7.5). A higher degree of Suppleness is required from the horse in this exercise as the loops are smaller (when ridden in a short arena) and there are more changes of bend.

Figure Eight with Transitions Over the Centerline (X)

Once the horse is confident at performing a figure eight, the rider can also consider including transitions within the figure eight.

At the lower levels of training the transitions could be simply trot – walk – trot (fig. 7.6). For horses at Second Level and above, a simple change canter – walk – canter would be suitable (fig. 7.7). And for the more advanced horses, such as those training at Fourth Level and above, this could become a flying change. Of course, the transitions should only be incorporated into these exercises once they are well established.

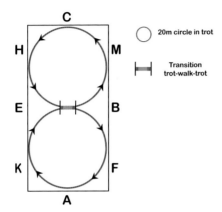

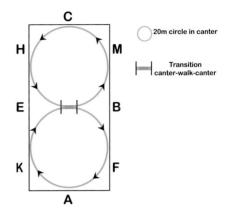

7.6

A figure eight ridden in trot with a transition to walk and back up to trot over the centerline. ▲

7.7

A figure eight in canter with a simple change transition (canter – walk – canter) over the centerline. ▲

Progressing the complexity further than the figure eight, the rider can choose to move on to riding serpentines.

Three-Looped Serpentines with Transitions Over the Centerline

As with the figure eight, the type of transition ridden will depend upon the horse's level of training. But whatever the level, the difficulty is increased by the fact that there are more changes of bend and more transitions within the exercise.

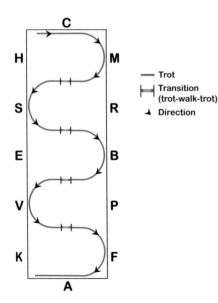

A five-looped serpentine ridden in trot with transitions to walk and back up to trot when crossing the centerline (A), and a visualization of the same serpentine transposed onto an arena to give a more realistic perspective (B). Of course, it is worth pointing out that the fifth loop is out of view as it was behind where the photographer was standing. ▲

Trot
Transition
(trot-walk-trot)
Direction

Five-Looped Serpentines with Transitions Over the Centerline

The five-looped serpentine is the next step up in difficulty. The bends are tighter and require an even higher degree of Suppleness. Moreover, as the turns all happen

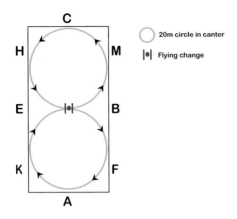

A

C

H   M

○ 20m circle in canter

|•| Flying change

E |•| B

K   F

A

B

7.9 A & B

A figure eight with a flying change over the centerline (A). This horse is just learning to do the flying changes, hence at this stage, he is able to do a single change over X, but is not yet ready to attempt anything more challenging (B). ▲

so much more quickly, the horse has to be well established in his work and able to change his bend and gait without losing the quality of all the training elements (figs. 7.8 A & B).

Finally, once the horse is able to complete a five-looped serpentine competently in trot, can perform 10-meter circles in canter, and is also confident with the flying changes, what can the rider do to continue his development to achieve the five-looped serpentine with flying changes? She could try riding:

- A figure eight with a flying change over the centerline (figs. 7.9 A & B).

- A three-looped serpentine with the flying changes.

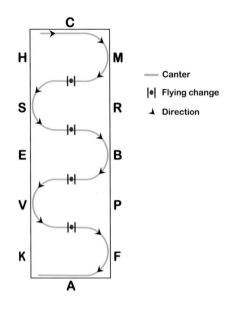

C

H   M

S   R

E   B

V   P

K   F

A

—— Canter

|•| Flying change

◢ Direction

7.10

The five-looped serpentine with flying changes
each time the horse crosses the centerline. ◢

- And if that is all going well, the five-looped serpentine with the flying changes each time the horse crosses the centerline (fig. 7.10).

Again, these steps will not happen in one session but over weeks, months, or years of training (Weekly, Monthly, and Yearly Spirals).

In this progressive exercise, you can see quite clearly how a complex and advanced movement is based upon mastery of a relatively simple one (the 20-meter circle) and how the movements gradually increase in difficulty as the horse moves up the Training Spiral (fig. 7.11). The importance of such foundation exercises should never be underestimated. Time and care should be put into establishing the basic foundations of a horse's training, yet all too often, this is rushed. Where this is the case, the horse may struggle physically or mentally with the higher levels of performance.

So what should you do if a horse runs into problems with the more advanced forms of an exercise? In chapter 3 (p. 44), we looked at the case of a horse experiencing difficulties at the higher levels of the Training Spiral and saw how a wise rider will take him a step (or two or three) back down before trying to re-ascend. The same applies here. When a horse is having problems with a more advanced exercise, take a step back to revisit the

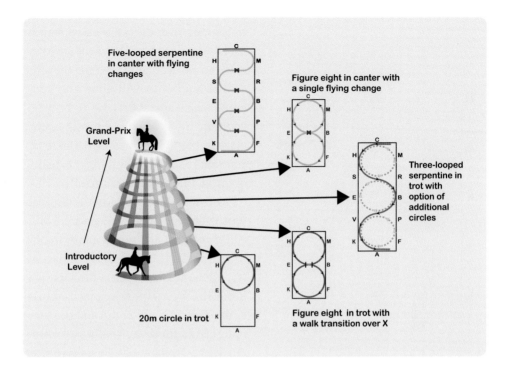

7.11

Visualization of where some of the exercises described would fit on a Training Spiral in terms of their progression in difficulty, building toward the five-looped serpentine with flying changes. ▲

same exercise in a more basic form. Once the quality has been re-established at this lower tier, the horse should be ready to have another go at the more difficult forms of the exercise.

Sometimes the rider will need to adapt the basic form of the exercise to develop the horse's skills in the direction required. For example, it may be that when riding a five-looped serpentine, the horse is always slow to change his bend to the right, and this causes him to fall in and thus lose Rhythm. When the rider returns to the simple figure eight, she finds that he can cope well with this, so moves back up to the three-looped serpentine. At this point, she notices that although the horse *can* cope with the three loops, he is a little slower to change his bend to the right and feels a bit stiffer on the right bends than the left.

By taking a step back, the rider has identified exactly what needs to be improved: to perform the five-looped serpentine, the horse has to be more supple to the right. With this knowledge, she can elaborate on the three-looped serpentine

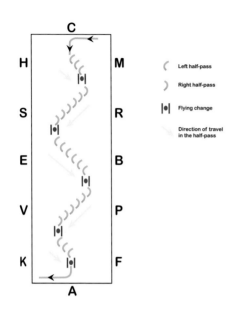

H · C · M

S · R

E · B

V · P

K · F

A

(Left half-pass

) Right half-pass

|•| Flying change

Direction of travel
in the half-pass

7.12

The Grand Prix canter zigzag. ▲

to help improve the horse's Suppleness. An obvious way forward would be to include an extra circle every time they ride a right loop. This will allow the horse more time to establish the right bend; additionally, as he will be bending more often to the right, it will help him to become more supple (assuming the quality of the additional circles is good).

Note that this is a typical learning pattern. Often, after attempting a more difficult movement and running into trouble with it, a rider will see only the surface effects of the problem, such as the horse falling in. However, if the rider goes back to an easier form of the exercise and the same thing occurs, the underlying causes will often become apparent. Problems are often easier to identify and correct when working at the lower level or in a slower gait.

★ Progressive Exercise 2 – From Turn-on-the-Forehand to Canter Zigzags

For our next example, let's look at how another advanced movement, the canter zigzag, can be developed from a very simple exercise—in this case, the turn-on-the-forehand.

For those unfamiliar with a canter zigzag, this is a very advanced movement in which the horse has to half-pass (move sideways in the direction he is bending) in canter, then perform a flying change

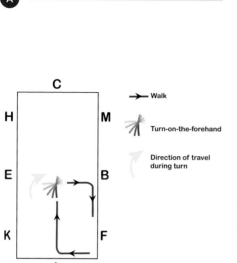

C

H   M

E   B

K   F

A

→ Walk

Turn-on-the-forehand

Direction of travel during turn

7.13 A–C

The turn-on-the-forehand (A), and a horse performing a turn-on-the-forehand, moving away from the rider's *right* leg. You can clearly see the horse's right hind leg crossing in front of the left hind leg (B). In another example, the horse is performing a turn-on-the-forehand away from the rider's *left* leg (C). Again, the inside hind leg can clearly be seen crossing over. ▲

and immediately half-pass in the other direction, then perform another flying change and half-pass in the original direction, and so on. In the Grand Prix dressage test, the horse is required to perform five half-passes to either side of centerline with flying changes of leg at each change of direction, the first half-pass to the left and the last to the left of three strides, the others of six strides (fig. 7.12). Phew! Hard enough to *read,* let alone ride!

Of course, to perform such a movement the horse has to be highly trained and well established with its two main elements—the canter half-pass and the flying change. But let's look back a bit further, to where his training would have started many years previously. At the most basic level, the horse would have been taught how to perform a turn-on-the-forehand (figs. 7.13 A–C). This is an exercise in which he is asked to

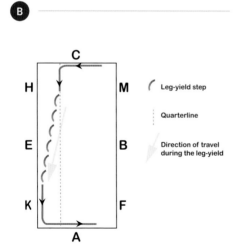

(B)

7.14 A & B
Leg-yield being performed from the quarterline to the track (A), and a visualization of it being performed within the context of the arena (B). ▲

move his hindquarters around his forehand—a good starting point for all kinds of lateral (sideways) work.

Next, we would introduce the leg-yield, in which the horse is asked to move simultaneously forward and sideways away from the direction in which he is bending.

The exercise has many variations. It can be performed on a straight line, for example, from the quarterline to the track (figs. 7.14 A & B), or in a circle spiraling outward (fig. 7.15). The leg-yield can be ridden at any gait. It is usually first taught in walk, then in trot, and eventually, can be performed in canter. In training, however, it is most often used in trot.

To begin with, the rider will want to initiate the leg-yield so it works with however the horse is already bent at the start of the exercise. That is to say, if the horse is already bending right, the rider will use her right leg to move the horse's body from that side to the left. To increase the difficulty, the rider can start from a left bend and perform a leg-yield moving the horse away from the right leg. This is more taxing because the horse will need to change the bend in his body just prior to performing the leg-yield.

Next, to add to the degree of difficulty, you can introduce a 10-meter circle before or after the leg-yield (fig. 7.16). Then this circle can be ridden in the opposite direction to the bend ridden in the leg-yield— that is, circle right, followed by a change of bend to the left, then leg-yield away from the rider's left leg (fig. 7.17). This will not only increase the difficulty even more, but also help to prepare the horse for traveling sideways then changing the bend to travel sideways in the opposite direction as in the canter zigzag.

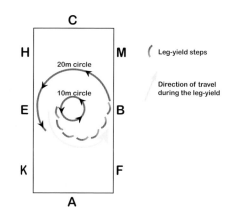

7.15

Leg-yield on a curved line, starting in a 10-meter circle and leg-yielding outward onto a 20-meter circle. ▲

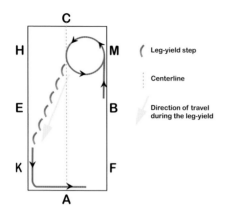

Leg-yield step

Centerline

Direction of travel
during the leg-yield

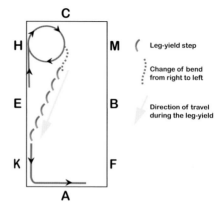

Leg-yield step

Change of bend
from right to left

Direction of travel
during the leg-yield

7.16

A circle in a *matching* direction to the leg-yield.
A 10-meter circle on the left rein is ridden
at M before being followed by the leg-yield
away from the rider's left leg so the horse travels
across the arena toward K. ▲

7.17

A circle in an *opposing* direction to the leg-yield.
A 10-meter circle right is ridden at H, followed
by a change of bend so the rider can ask the
horse to leg-yield away from her left leg so
the horse travels across the arena toward K. ▲

To further increase the level of difficulty, the rider can ride a leg-yield zigzag.
That is, she can leg-yield a few steps in
one direction, then change the horse's
bend and leg-yield a few steps in the other
(fig. 7.18). This should only be attempted
when the horse is well established with
the basic form of a leg-yield.

Once the zigzag is mastered, the horse
will have the concept of traveling sideways, changing the bend, and traveling
sideways in the other direction. This,
plainly, is the basis of the canter half-
pass zigzag. But to perform this advanced

movement, the horse will have to learn other elements, most obviously the flying changes and the half-pass.

Remember, I won't go into great detail about how to train the horse to perform each movement. Of the flying change, suffice to say that the training of this movement starts with the canter – trot – canter transition, progresses to the simple change canter – walk – canter, before becoming the flying change canter left – canter right or vice versa. There are many other exercises that will need to be performed to increase the horse's general ability to perform the flying change.

The progressive steps to training the half-pass can be outlined as follows: Once the horse is competent with the leg-yield, the next step is learning the shoulder-in. This can be taught in various ways. One way of teaching the horse the shoulder-in is by riding a 10-meter circle, then incorporating the leg-yield on the first step of the circle, thus leg-yielding the circle along the track (fig. 7.19 A).

The aim of the shoulder-in is for the horse to be able to bend around the rider's inside leg and to hold this bend while traveling in a forward direction so the shoulders are placed on the inner track and the hindquarters remain on the outer track (figs. 7.19 B & C). More precisely, he should now be working on three tracks—that is, inside foreleg on one track, outside foreleg and inside hind leg on the middle track, and

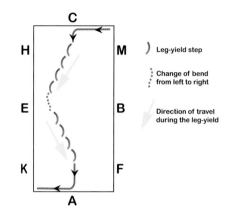

) Leg-yield step

⋮ Change of bend
  from left to right

Direction of travel
during the leg-yield

7.18

A leg-yield with a change of direction (the zigzag). Starting on the left rein and turning down the centerline, the rider first moves the horse away from her left leg for several steps, then changes the horse's bend before moving him away from her right leg to return to the centerline again. Since she has changed the bend, the rider will turn right at A, as this is matching the horse's bend in the last leg-yield. ▲

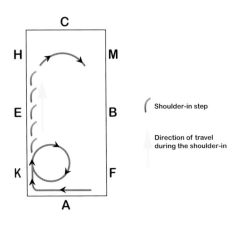

Shoulder-in step

Direction of travel
during the shoulder-in

7.19 A–C

To train the shoulder-in, begin with a 10-meter circle right ridden at K. While maintaining the bend of the circle, the horse is asked to move away from the right leg in a similar manner as with a leg-yield in (A). In (B), you see a horse performing a shoulder-in on the long side of the arena with a visualization of where the following steps would be marked by the red and blue lines. Notice how the horse is working on three tracks. In (C) we get the shoulder-in from a different angle. It clearly shows the bend in the horse's body around the rider's inside leg and how the movement is both forward and sideways. You can see that despite bending and working on three tracks, the horse is still Straight—that is, he has good alignment throughout his body and neck. ▲

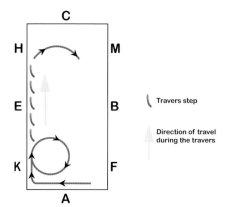

Travers step

Direction of travel
during the travers

7.20 A & B

Travers, shown in (A), is ridden in a similar
pattern to the shoulder-in, but this time the
haunches are placed on the inner track as
opposed to the shoulders. In (B) you can see
a horse performing travers with a visualization
of the previous steps the horse has already
taken in the travers. Again, you can see
how the horse is working on three tracks,
but this time, the inside hind is on the
innermost track, and the outside foreleg
is on the outermost track. ▲

outside hind leg on the outer track. This
movement is maintained for a few steps,
then the horse can exit the shoulder-in by
moving forward onto a curved line.

The movement known as travers
(haunches-in) is the next step in the
training. For this movement, the horse
should travel down the long side with
his hindquarters on the inner track (figs.
7.20 A & B).

The shoulder-in and travers form the
basis of the half-pass (figs. 7.21 A & B).
Indeed, often trainers will describe a half-
pass as being very similar if not the same as
a travers across a diagonal line (fig. 7.22).

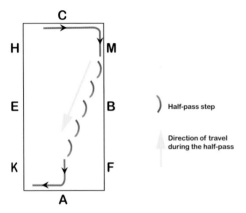

$)$ Half-pass step

$\uparrow$ Direction of travel during the half-pass

7.21 A & B

Half-pass: In (A) the horse would be traveling on the right rein in trot and at M would begin the half-pass steps toward the centerline, bending in the same direction he is traveling in. In (B) we see the half-pass with a visualization as to the horse's next steps. We can clearly see how the horse is bending in the direction in which he is traveling. ▲

Once the horse is happy with a straightforward half-pass in trot (and canter) from the centerline to the track, the rider can consider increasing the difficulty. As with the leg-yield exercises, one option would be to add in a 10-meter circle after half-passing in trot from the track to the centerline (figs. 7.23 A & B). The circle could have the opposite bend to that of the half-pass, requiring the horse to change his bend immediately on hitting the centerline. If the horse has a clear understanding of the concept of zigzag in trot, it will help him to grasp the canter zigzag. Of course, the latter is

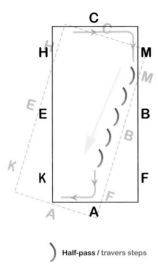

) **Half-pass** / travers steps

If we imagine the arena wall is now across a diagonal line, then the half-pass steps are the equivalent to travers.

7.22

We can see how the half-pass is the same as the travers if we tilt the arena onto a diagonal angle. ◄

7.23 A & B

Half-pass followed by circle. In (A), the horse starts on the left rein and at H performs a half-pass to X where he then changes the bend and travels on a 10-meter circle to the right to establish the new bend, then performs a half-pass right from X to K. For this exercise the horse needs to emphasize the sideways movement more in order to reach the centerline by X. In (B) you can see how the horse is crossing his legs more to create an increased sideways element to the half-pass. ▼

A

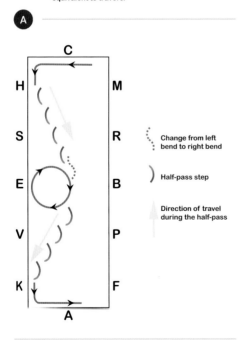

Change from left bend to right bend

) Half-pass step

Direction of travel during the half-pass

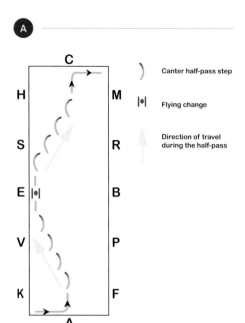

A

C → →

H   M   )   Canter half-pass step

S   R |•| Flying change

                                 Direction of travel
E |•| B   during the half-pass

V   P

K   F

A

B

7.24 A & B

In (A) we see a half-pass in canter with one flying change. The horse starts in left canter on the left rein and turns down the centerline at A, then performs a half-pass left to E, where he performs a flying change and proceeds straight away to half-pass right to G so he can turn right at C. In (B), the horse is cantering in a left half-pass toward the track in preparation for the flying change. You can see how his body is bending to the left and how he is crossing his legs as he travels to the left. ▲

more challenging because of the need to change the canter lead as well.

If you assume the horse is also now well established in the flying changes, then a further possibility is to ride the canter half-pass from the centerline to the track, and follow this with a flying change (figs. 7.24 A & B).

In canter, the zigzag is best introduced as a few steps of half-pass one way; straighten up; the flying change; and finally, a few steps of half-pass the other way. This can then be built up gradually until the horse can perform the six strides one way (flying change), six strides the other way sequence as required in the Grand Prix test (figs. 7.25 A–C).

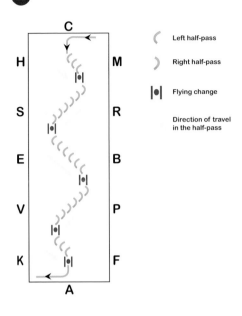

Left half-pass

Right half-pass

Flying change

Direction of travel
in the half-pass

7.25 A–C

The canter zigzag: In (A), the horse starts on
the left rein in canter, turns down the centerline,
then performs five half-passes to either side of
centerline with a flying change of leg at each
change of direction—the first half-pass to the
left and the last to the left of three strides,
the others of six strides. In (B) you can see
the moment in which the horse has completed
the right half-pass (visualized by the three
steps of right half-pass) and is performing the
flying change before continuing in left half-pass
(visualized by the three steps of left half-pass
shown near the bottom of the image). In (C)
we see the same movement being performed in B,
but this time from the side in the moment
the horse is performing the flying change. ▲

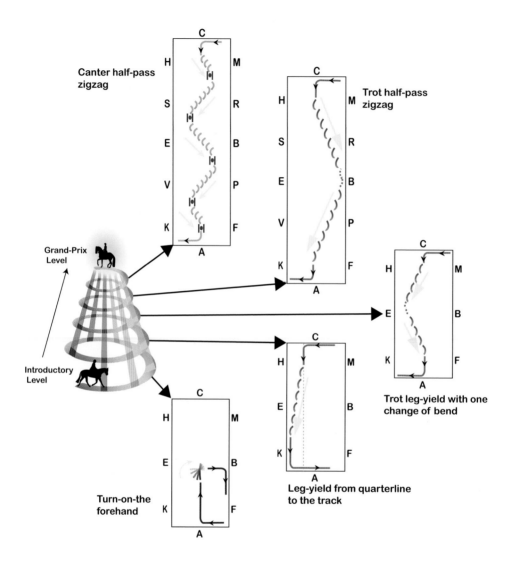

Canter half-pass
zigzag

Trot half-pass
zigzag

Grand-Prix
Level

Introductory
Level

Trot leg-yield with one
change of bend

Turn-on-the
forehand

Leg-yield from quarterline
to the track

7.26

Where some of the movements described would fit on the Training Spiral
in terms of their progression in difficulty, building toward the Grand Prix canter zigzag. ▲

Again, you can see how the exercises progress in difficulty and complexity from one level to the next, yet it should not be forgotten that the more basic exercises always form the foundation of even the most complex ones (fig. 7.26).

This is just a glimpse into how an advanced movement has at its foundation the basic movements. There are, of course, many more movements than the ones shown here that the horse and rider will need to practice in order to progress to the higher levels. As I said at the beginning, the aim of this chapter was not to provide a comprehensive guide but to show how a rider can link a series of progressively more difficult movements to develop from one level to the next. To do this successfully, the rider needs to understand the movements, know how to ride them, and have a sense of the problems that are commonly encountered at each stage. Most riders benefit from working with a good coach to help with this.

Above all, I want to encourage the idea of looking at the bigger picture when training the horse. The "big picture approach" has several huge benefits:

- It has, at its core, a vision of progress, based on the idea that movement to the higher tiers on the Spiral and levels of training is always possible.

- It enables a more accurate perception of the level the rider and horse are currently at in their training.

- It fosters a deeper understanding of the level at which they are training, based on a knowledge of the more advanced movements.

- It encourages and enables progression to the next tier or level.

end of chapter 7

Exercise Development—The Progressive Vision

> *Ultimately, it is up to you
> as the rider to learn
> which tool is best to use when.*

chapter

8

Case Studies

n this final chapter, I want to explore a number of real-life situations that I have experienced during coaching sessions, looking in detail at both the problems that arose and the solutions that we found. The cases have been selected because they strike me as both typical and revealing and are exactly the kinds of scenarios that coaches and riders often encounter during training.

★ Case 1: First Level

This story involves a rider on a horse that has hacked a lot but remains fairly inexperienced in terms of his formal schooling and they are working at First Level. The rider works regularly with a coach who uses the Training Spiral concept, so the rider is familiar with it.

After an initial warm-up, the coach asks, "How is your horse working for you today?"

☺ RIDER: "He is picking up trot very well today, but once in the trot he is speeding up on the long sides and going slow on the short sides of the arena. He is leaning on my reins, and he feels quite rigid in his neck."

★ COACH: "So what are the elements that you need to work on improving right now?"

☺ RIDER: "Let's see, there is a lack of rhythm in the trot, he is not good in the rein contact, and his neck is stiff. So Rhythm, Contact, and Suppleness would be the three elements needing to be improved."

★ COACH: "That's right. But which of them do you think is the number one priority to work on?"

☺ RIDER: "Well, it should be the Rhythm, as that is the starting point of the Spiral."

★ COACH: "Yes, that's right—but why would you not want to improve his Contact first?"

☺ RIDER: "I'm not exactly sure, but in the past when he was working like this and I tried to get him lighter into my hand, he just began to get even heavier on my hand and even faster down the long sides of the arena."

★ COACH: "I bet he gets tighter in his neck, too?"

☺ RIDER: "Yes, he does! But why?"

★ COACH: "This is because, as you said earlier, Rhythm is at the bottom of the Tower and is the starting point of the Spiral. It sounds as though you have been trying to work on the Contact before having a suitable degree of Rhythm and Suppleness. As a result, the Tower crumbles and then the Rhythm and Suppleness that you had deteriorates."

☺ RIDER: "That makes sense."

★ COACH: "Good, so let's do some work to improve his Rhythm."

They ride some transitions within the trot, to help the rider get more control over the regularity. This also provides the horse with more opportunities to learn what the signals are, and what response the rider is looking for from each one. Each time the horse does a good transition, the rider provides him with clear feedback, indicating that his response was acceptable. In this case, the rider pats him and uses her voice to tell him that he is good.

But what do we do when the horse's responses to the transition aids are *not* acceptable? In the first place, the rider should repeat the aids but a little more strongly, to indicate that he did not react to the earlier signals appropriately. The rider should then repeat the transition, to give her horse another chance to find the desired response. On occasions, she may have to do this several times before he gets it right without the repeated signals. As always, it is important for the horse that he is given enough opportunities to learn what is being asked.

☺RIDER: "Why do we need to keep repeating these transitions until he gets them right?"

★ COACH: "If he performs a transition that is not acceptable and you correct him by asking again with stronger aids, then although he may perform the transition okay in the end, he will be left in the situation of understanding what is *not* an acceptable response. He is still none the wiser as to what is actually acceptable; it is not until he gets it 'right,' and you reward him, that he has a real understanding of what is acceptable as well as what is not. Of course, we also have to allow him many of these 'learning opportunities' before he will have an established knowledge base of what is required."

☺RIDER: "So, it's about letting him practice, and if he gets it wrong, not worrying about it but gently letting him know it's wrong, then repeating, so he can find the right answer, and telling him each time he gets it right."

★ COACH: "Exactly."

They practice some more, and before long, the horse is beginning to understand the signals better and is able to maintain a much more regular Rhythm all the way around the arena. The rider finds she is able to give more subtle signals to correct the Rhythm, as the horse begins to understand what is required of him.

★ **COACH:** "So now you feel his Rhythm is much more regular, what would be your next priority to work on?"

☺ RIDER: "That would be Suppleness."

★ **COACH:** "Yes, how does his Suppleness feel now?"

☺ RIDER: "It is better than at the start—his neck feels much less rigid."

★ **COACH:** "That's good. He is probably less rigid in his body now that he is not continually speeding up, or falling forward and slowing down, or dropping behind your leg—in other words 'getting lazy.' The loss of Rhythm would also cause a loss of balance, which would likewise cause him to become tight in his body. But do you think his neck could be even softer?"

☺ RIDER: "Yes, there is still some tightness in it, I think."

★ **COACH:** "So ask him to do some neck-flexing exercises—but make sure you keep noticing the quality of his Rhythm, and if you need to at any point, leave the neck flexing and return to your Rhythm exercises."

Her horse continues to maintain a good Rhythm as she adds some neck-flexing exercises.

☺ RIDER: "That's better, he feels much softer in his neck, and in fact, through his whole body now."

★ **COACH:** "That is good—he is now much more supple. Assuming he maintains a good Rhythm and this degree of Suppleness, what are you going to focus on next?"

☺ RIDER: "The Contact?"

★ COACH: "Absolutely. How does his Contact feel at the moment?"

☺ RIDER: "Well, it is much lighter than it was at the start; actually, it's really nice now as he feels softer in the Contact but not overly light and dropping the reins."

★ COACH: "Yes, I can see that. This is because you have built a good foundation and he is now able to carry himself in a balanced way and is working forward and relaxed. Also, doing the neck-flexing exercises has loosened him so that he is now able to be softer into your Contact. Well done!"

At this point, we can allow the horse and rider in this case study to have a little rest while we summarize their progress: They had three elements they wanted to work on: the Rhythm, the Suppleness, and the Contact.

They worked first on the Rhythm, and once it had improved a degree, they moved on to the Suppleness; however, they were prepared at any point to return to the Rhythm as their priority if needed. Having worked on these two elements, it became clear that the quality of the Contact had *already* improved, simply from working on Rhythm and Suppleness.

After a break, horse and rider picked the work back up again and rebuilt the quality they had before. Then they progressed on to developing a little more Impulsion in the work by riding some transitions from trot to canter. After this, they worked on Straightness by riding some straight lines down the centerline and by riding some 20-meter and then 15-meter circles. By the end of the session, the pair had worked on all of the elements and the horse was working with an improved degree of collection as well as being less on his forehand and working with more engagement in his hindquarters.

This case study involves a horse who is well established at Second Level and progressing toward Third. At this point we would expect him to have a good degree of Rhythm, Suppleness, Contact, and so on, and to be in the process of moving up through his Yearly Training Spiral.

As this is the first time the coach has seen this horse working, she asks the rider to go through the sort of warm-up they'd normally do, just so she can observe them working together.

As the horse warms up, he shows a good degree of Rhythm in all three gaits and is clearly able to stretch and work in a longer and lower outline, as well as in a working frame. In other words, he is showing a good degree of Suppleness and is working forward into an accepting Contact. All is looking good and progressing well so far in the Daily Training Spiral.

With the horse nicely warmed up, the rider begins to develop the exercises and they ride some leg-yield. At this point, it becomes clear that the horse is moving away from the left leg better than he is from the right; moreover, he is falling through his outside shoulder when performing the leg-yield—and this, too, is particularly noticeable to the right.

The rider then works on some variations within the gaits. The horse shows some potentially very expressive medium trot strides to begin with, but then loses his Rhythm and begins to run. By now the coach has had a good opportunity to assess the horse's basic way of going, and the rider has been able to warm him up and get a feel for how he is working today. The coach, therefore, asks the rider to give the horse a short break.

★ **COACH:** "Okay, that was a good, well-structured warm-up you did there. So, tell me what you felt was going on—and how it compares to the way your horse normally works for you."

☺ RIDER: "This is pretty much how he normally works. I always feel his leg-yield on the right is harder than on the left, and he always ends up running in the medium trots. This is something I always lose marks for in my dressage tests."

★ **COACH:** "Okay, I would agree with that from what I saw. Do you know why he always ends up running in his medium trots? As I'm sure you can feel, he starts off well and looks as though he has the scope to produce a lovely medium trot."

☺ RIDER: "I'm not really sure—it's like he just loses his balance, then runs faster, and by the time we are at the other end of the arena it has all fallen apart. It takes us the whole of the short side to get it back together again."

★ **COACH:** "Yes, but it is actually coming from a lack of Straightness in his body. What he is doing in his medium trot is similar to the problem with the leg-yield: he is falling (or spilling) through his outside shoulder. In the medium trot he starts well but then it begins to go wrong—with each step he is falling a little more through that outside shoulder until he is crooked (not straight) and this causes him to be out of balance. He then needs to take shorter but quicker steps to regain his balance—and this is the point at which you feel he is now running, or losing his Rhythm."

☺ RIDER: "Oh, I've never noticed that. I mean, I'm aware of him falling out in the leg-yield, but never noticed it in the medium trots."

★ **COACH:** "Well let's go out and try again—but first we'll ride some exercises to gain more control over the shoulders. This should give you a clearer means of telling him how to straighten his body—and not to fall out through that shoulder."

The rider takes the horse back out and begins working some turn-on-the-haunches or walk pirouettes in order to gain more control over the horse's shoulders. The exercise helps the horse become more aware of how he is positioning his body, and thus of his alignment or Straightness. After a few of these turns in each direction, they go back to work on the leg-yielding—but with an increased awareness of the Straightness within the movement.

The rider is now able to "'catch" the horse's shoulder before he is falling out too much, and to correct it. One particularly useful exercise that they perform at this point is the "staircase" leg-yield (fig. 8.1). Like the turns-on-the-haunches or walk pirouettes, this helps the horse to become more aware of his own body positioning, and consequently to maintain a much better degree of Straightness through the movements.

★ **COACH:** "How is it going? Do you feel more aware of how and when your horse is losing his Straightness through the shoulder? And do you feel more able to correct this?"
☺ RIDER: "I had not realized before quite how much he was drifting out though his outside shoulder. It now feels as though he is maintaining a much better quality throughout his leg-yield, rather than it fading toward the end. Why is that?"

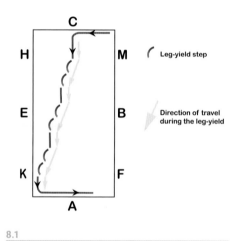

8.1

The staircase leg-yield exercise. ▲

The coach takes a moment to explain the Training Spiral—the way in which each element is built on the next, and how the whole sequence repeats at the next tier up. In this case, the horse lost the degree of Straightness required at the lower tier, meaning that the elements above all fell apart.

With this in mind, the horse and rider go back to work on the medium trot. The coach asks the rider to perform a medium trot down the quarterline and to be very aware of any loss of Straightness.

☺ RIDER: "Ah, yes, now I can really feel how he wants to drift through the outside shoulder as the trot gets bigger. I am trying to correct it with my outside rein, but it still feels like he is falling a little bit through the shoulder."

★ COACH: "Great, you are halfway there now! Once you are aware of it, you can start to correct it. Try asking for the medium trot down the quarterline again, but this time add in a little neck flexion to the outside, to help to straighten him even more."

☺ RIDER: "That was better—he felt like he kept the same quality through the whole thing there."

★ COACH: "That's looking much better now. There are various techniques that you can use to straighten him—for example, the counter-bend (bending a little to the outside) or 'catching' his outside shoulder. A shoulder-in or shoulder-fore (small angle of shoulder-in) may also help. Are you familiar with all of these?"

☺ RIDER: "Yes, I'm quite happy riding all of them."

★ COACH: "Good—so now it is up to you, as the rider, to experiment a bit with these different techniques. You need to get a feel for the one that works best to straighten your horse in any given situation.

This is actually an important point. A coach can give you the tools (techniques and exercises), but ultimately it is up to you, as rider, to learn which tool is best to use when. This will often come through experimentation. You will be much better equipped to select an appropriate tool if you understand *why* a coach might suggest that particular exercise in the situation—and *how* the exercise works.

☺RIDER: "I remember when he was younger, I always had a problem with him falling out through that right shoulder, even on his 20-meter circles. But I really thought I had fixed that."

★ COACH: "This is where training is very much a Spiral; you need to accept that you will revisit each of the six elements of the Scales of Training many times. Every horse will have a particular weakness, and it is likely this will reappear at each level of training. I'm sure you *did* fix the Straightness issues you encountered when he was younger, and he can now perform a 20-meter circle with a good degree of Straightness. However, now you have moved upward on the Spiral, the Straightness issues have reemerged—but this time within the more advanced movements, such as the leg-yield and the medium trots. You will probably find that as his training develops even further, and he progresses up the Spiral, that issues with Straightness will surface once again."

☺RIDER: "That all makes sense. Also, I'm thinking that this could explain why my marks in the dressage tests are always better for the shoulder-in to the right than they are to the left. Is he falling out more through that outside shoulder in the left shoulder-in, just as he was in the leg-yield?"

★ COACH: "Yes, that is very likely. It's great that you are linking all this together now. In our next session, we can take a look at the shoulder-in, but in the meantime, you can continue to work him the way you have been, as his basic way of working is really good. However, as we have discovered, you always need to be more aware of the Straightness issue."

In this coaching session, we can clearly see how the weaknesses in a particular element of the Scales of Training can resurface at a new tier of the Training Spiral, even when the rider has already worked on that element and developed a good quality of it within their horse at a lower levels of training (fig. 8.2).

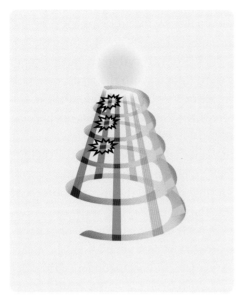

8.2

As we learn in this case study, horse and rider revisit weaknesses—in this story, Straightness—as they resurface at higher tiers of the Spiral. At the lower tiers of the Spiral, Straightness is well established. ▲

In this final case study, we look at a Fourth Level horse and rider attempting one of the more demanding exercises at this higher level of training. The coach works with them every two weeks, so knows both horse and rider quite well.

The horse is well established at Third Level and is beginning to work on movements such as the tempi changes (several flying changes performed in a row, with a set number of canter strides in between). The rider has said that she is having a problem here, as when she asks for the "four times" (four canter strides between each flying change) sometimes her horse will change on the fourth stride but at other times it will be on the fifth or even sixth stride.

> ★ **COACH:** "Go and have a warm up, and when he is ready, I'd like you to show me some individual flying changes so we can just check the quality of those before we look at the tempi changes."

The rider warms up her horse and the coach notes that he shows a good quality of Rhythm in all his gaits, including the transitions from collected to medium paces. She then works the horse with some exercises to improve his Suppleness, including leg-yielding and shoulder-in. She also intermittently brings him down into a long, low frame to stretch him over his back. So far everything is looking good: He has a nice, light, yet forward Contact into the reins, meaning that the rider is able to put more energy into his work, while at the same time he maintains a consistent Rhythm and does not become stronger or braced in his body.

The coach then asks the rider to perform some transitions on a line away from the track, to check the horse's Straightness. This seems to be okay when they perform the trot to canter, but a little crookedness becomes apparent in the walk to canter. The same lack of Straightness appears in the individual flying changes. As the problem is only very slight and does not have a huge impact upon the overall quality at this stage, the coach wonders if the rider is aware of it.

★ **COACH:** "How straight do you think he is as you ride the walk-to-canter transitions and the flying change?"

☺RIDER: "I am aware that he is curling his body a bit, but only as we ride the transitions. Before and after that he feels pretty straight."

★ **COACH:** "It is good that you are aware of this, as it is something that we will need to address. Otherwise, everything is looking very good. Now, I would like you to go and ride your tempi changes, with a flying change every fourth stride."

The rider performs a few tempi changes. It now becomes apparent that although the horse is trying to respond to her signals at the correct point (every fourth stride), it sometimes takes him another stride or two to get organized enough to actually perform the change.

★ **COACH:** "Okay, so how did they go?"

☺RIDER: "That's about what I have been getting from him. I feel the first couple of changes work okay, then they get progressively worse, and it's like he just doesn't listen to my aids. It is as though he just switches off."

★ **COACH:** "So do you feel like it is a problem with the quality of his acceptance and reaction to your leg? In other words, with the quality of the Contact, but in this case, not necessarily the rein contact?"

☺RIDER: "Yes, it's like he is just being lazy."

★ **COACH:** "But when you ask for the third and the fourth changes, do you feel he is trying to do something for you?"

☺RIDER: "Well, I guess he is—but as he begins to come up more in his body, he will do a stride or two of a slightly more bouncy canter before he finally gets the change."

★ **COACH:** "So is he just being lazy and ignoring your signals— or is it that his body is not in a position where he has enough Rhythm, Suppleness, Contact, Impulsion, Straightness, and Collection in order to be able to perform the changes?"

☺RIDER: "Hmm...I guess the quality of the canter steps between the changes isn't as good as before we start them."

★ **COACH:** "Now you are on the right track! You have a good quality of canter before you ride the first change, but then a hint of crookedness creeps in as he changes. When you are riding a single change, you find you can fix that and straighten him within a couple of steps—but when you are riding a line of changes, this little bit of crookedness can go uncorrected because you are focused on the next change. I don't know if you've noticed, but in the canter steps between the changes, his Impulsion also decreases. That is why you feel he has to almost gather himself together again, before he can actually do the changes for you."

☺RIDER: "You are right: I am not thinking about the quality of the canter between the changes, I am too busy just trying to count the steps and get my legs in the right place to be able to ask for the next one!"

★COACH: "Let's go and ride some more changes, but this time, instead of riding them every four steps, make it every eight. That way you will have more time to focus on the quality of the canter between the changes."

This time the horse shows much more Straightness as the rider has more time to correct the quality of the canter and any crookedness that creeps in between the changes. They are able to perform the changes every eight strides.

☺RIDER: "So he wasn't just ignoring my leg then!"

★COACH: "No. What happened is that you lost the Impulsion at the lower tier of your Daily Spiral—a lower tier of the Tower—which resulted in all the elements above that crumbling. Now what you need to work on is multitasking. You need to be able to count the strides without losing awareness of all the other elements that need to be in place. This isn't easy! It's important that you ask one thing of your horse at a time—but as you speed up your reactions and he learns to respond more quickly to your signals, then within the four strides of canter you have between the changes, you should be able to check and correct all these elements. At the moment, the key thing to correct is the Impulsion, since this is the element you are losing and without the necessary degree of this element you will not be able to achieve the Straightness."

The rider rides another couple of lines of changes, this time with just six strides between. Most of the changes work well, but there is one in which the horse is a stride late.

☺RIDER: "I could feel that time how I lost the Impulsion and Straightness in the canter, just before that change where he was a stride late. I just need to become quicker at identifying and correcting it, don't I?"

★ COACH: "Yes! It's great that you are now more aware of the quality, or loss of it, in the canter between the changes. The important thing to remember is, if it all falls apart, don't just assume your horse isn't trying. He is a very willing horse! Instead, try to work out what elements are missing from the work and rebuild them one at a time. In the case of these tempi changes, however, you need to be able to rebuild them pretty quickly—and that can take a bit of practice, for both you and your horse." _

end of chapter 8

Case Studies

THE TRAINING SPIRAL

IN CONC

LUSION

Throughout this book, I have shown how the Scales of Training can provide a good basis for riders to create their own list of priorities when riding and also how the progression from one element of the Scales of Training to the next needs to be repeated throughout the horse's training.

Training should always be progressive and with the horse's well-being at its heart. To this end, the need for clear communication with your horse is of the utmost importance. As you have seen, a lack of communication or asking questions of your horse that he does not yet understand only leads to confusion for the horse and frustration between the horse and rider. Understanding how horses learn and progress is also a crucial part of being able to work with them and train them. We have seen how often horses can have recurring weaknesses in one particular element and how this will resurface at every tier of the Training Spiral. When riders do not understand that this is a normal part of a horse's progress, they can easily become disheartened or even feel that they have not achieved any progress training their horse, when in fact the exact opposite is true. The continuing need to develop the complexity of the movements as a horse progresses up the Training Spiral not only supports the progressive training of the horse but also prevents any stagnation or boredom from

IN CONC

LUSION

repeating the same exercises day in and day out. This is often what happens when a rider becomes stuck at a particular level. Riders become stuck at a level because their expectation of what they or their horses can achieve has been limited either by themselves or by others around them who have imposed their beliefs on them.

Having a clear vision of the path in front and how to progress in small simple steps is the key to being able to achieve this progress. Remember to keep the questions simple enough for you and your horse to understand and in the correct order: Rhythm, Suppleness, Contact, Impulsion, Straightness, and Collection.

Above all both you and your horse should enjoy the training process and with a lot of hard work and determination, you can both achieve more than you realize!

It just remains for me to say:
Happy and successful training!

I would like to acknowledge all the fantastic coaches and trainers who have inspired and educated me throughout my career.

Thanks also goes to my friends Kirsty, Jillian, and Sara for their support and encouragement throughout the process of writing this book.

Lastly, a huge thanks goes to Andy for all his ongoing and endless support for all my equestrian endeavors.

INDEX